9/24

The TV Arab

THE TV ARAB

Jack G. Shaheen

Bowling Green State University Popular Press
Bowling Green, Ohio 43403

Acknowledgements

My deepest gratitude to Richard Millett, Robert Duncan, Paul Tang and Judith Valente, who provided continual guidance. Thanks are also due David Brown, James Conniff, Jack Hayes, Vaughnie Lindsay, James Landers, Jane Millar, Dick Richmond, Kathy Sullivan, Richard Wilber and Kamil Winter for their generous assistance. I wish to thank Donna Mohme, Karyn Posner and Patricia Riggins for typing the manuscript.

Special thanks to these producers, writers and government and network officials in Los Angeles, New York and Washington: Don Bay, Harve Bennett, Clare O'Brien, Donn O'Brien, Don Brinkley, Bob Carroll, Jr., Virginia Carter, Cy Chermack, Malcolm Clarke, Madelyn Davis, Frank Glicksman, Jack Guss, Bettye King Hoffmann, Julie T. Hoover, Tom Kersey, Helen Loukas, Edward Palmer, Irving Pearlberg, Alan Rafkin, Meta Rosenberg, Bob Saidenberg, Van Gordon Sauter, Anthony Spinner, Jerome Stanley, Howard Stringer and John Wallach.

I am especially grateful to Michael and Michele, whose youthful presence gave me encouragement.

Jack G. Shaheen

**To Bernice
With Love**

Contents

Foreword

Television creates lasting images. Thus, we in the television news business have a greater responsibility than most to avoid stereotyping, whatever the ethnic background or racial origin of the people involved.

Dr. Jack Shaheen has studied the image of the Arabs that television has projected over the years and found us lacking. His well-documented and perceptive account finds a stereotyping that should concern us all. Too few people these days take the time to read newspapers and magazines. Most of us depend on television for the news.

When our view is clouded with the stereotypical images, it can have a profound effect on our perception of people and their problems.

Fortunately, there are cases where television news is showing the way.

Dr. Shaheen's book will be a valuable passport to objectivity in the future treatment of the Arab.

Ed Bradley

Introduction

Much of my philosophy about stereotyping stems from what I learned as a child from my mother, Nazara, and my grandparents, Naffa and Jacob Jacob. Their origins were in Lebanon, an Arab country with a rich heritage of ethnic and religious diversity. Our home in the steel city of Clairton, Pennsylvania, was a center for ethnic sharing—food, conversation, traditions and sometimes tears for those friends and relatives left behind in the "old country." The neighborhood consisted of people named Patellis, Mesco, Henderson, Geletko and Drnach, and was more like a family. We exchanged food—Arabic meat pies for sausage and lasagna. We exchanged thoughts—"Truman acts like a Republican"—and respect—"Your priest is a good man." It was a happy, innocent time.

During the post-war period most of the men were employed at the Clairton Works, one of the world's largest coke producing facilities. Flakes of coke dust speckled the sky daily, resting on windows, porches and cars. Sometimes they would filter into the homes to settle on potted plants and waxed floors. In Clairton, coke was a symbol of income, not pollution. Like most women in Clairton, my mother and grandmother worked at home doing the wash, darning socks and knitting afghans, raising children and trying endlessly to rid the rooms of the black flakes.

My mother did this and more. As a school janitress, she reported to work before sunrise. She scrubbed floors for children instead of teaching them, as her son later would. Mother loved going to school but her education came to a stop after the seventh grade. She was needed at home to care for six young brothers and sisters. Becoming a school teacher was more important to her than anything—except the family. Her love and the devotion of my grandparents kept me, for a time, innocent of prejudice. Stereotyping? I never heard of it.

We didn't have Little League in those days. We had a sandlot team

1

of sorts called the Cemetery Gravediggers, since we played next to the cemetery a few feet from the tombstones. The gravediggers never bothered us, but a neighbor sometimes called the police to chase us off. Our opposing teams were black or white, and sometimes mixed. We didn't have Orientals or Hispanics in Clairton. One all-black team always gave the Gravediggers a tussle. To us they were a team, not a black team. We went to the same school, shared the same friends and fought the same bullies. But on the field it was war. We tore into each other. After a game, nursing our bruises, we'd plot an escape route through the tombstones and into the weeds in case the cops showed up. There was always a rematch. As kids, we were playing, not fighting.

When I was six, my grandfather introduced me to a salesman at the Dinowitz's store—a Jew. Like "stereotype," Jew was a word that had no meaning for me. And it was not until I grew up that I learned the meaning of the words "kike" and "nigger." Dinowitz's clothing shop was in Pittsburgh, about sixteen miles from Clairton. At the beginning and end of each school year, Grandfather would take me in for new clothes. I couldn't understand why he took me there. It seemed to me that he and the salesman disliked each other. They always yelled and waved their hands—a form of communication, I learned later, that is characteristically ethnic, a delightful expression of people who live close to their emotions. At first, these gyrations scared me. When I found out it was just a game, a fun way of doing business, these scenes became something I looked forward to. On occasion, I still try to barter when I go shopping. But yellow tags, not flamboyant words and gestures, determine the final price.

It would take only minutes for my grandfather to select and pay for my clothes. Then he and the salesman would talk and drink coffee for hours. I didn't mind waiting. Being around grown-ups was special, particularly when you were bribed with Coke and a candy bar. Grandfather also introduced me to other friends, such as the Campolongo family. Mrs. Campolongo always shared her fresh Italian bread and tasty spaghetti. Despite the fact I was only in my early teens Mr. Campolongo would cautiously emerge from his basement with a small glass of home-made wine. "Here, Jackie," he'd whisper. "for you. You like?"

"Yes," I would say. "I like."

As a steelworker and peddler, my grandfather Jacob easily entered the mainstream of American social and economic life. His peddling gave him personal contact and warm relationships with fellow Americans. Self-taught English lessons began with scribbled phrases on his white cuffs: "This is the best." "Want to save money?" "I give you credit." When he came to a doorstep with his brown peddler's pack, everyone welcomed him—black, white, Jew and Gentile. Grandfather was a fixture in Clairton.

These are fond reflections of the past—the early 1940s through the mid-1950s. For me it was a time when trust took precedence over profit. Today anonymous clerks in shopping malls have replaced the peddler's personal touch. We no longer engage in colorful bargaining. Nor do we see wrinkled brown packages of fine linen and household wares held together by knotted strands of twine. The human touch of the peddler is gone. Now we have discount stores with fixed prices and food wrapped in plastic. Credit cards replace handshakes.

As a working, middle-class family living on the outskirts of Pittsburgh, we never experienced the sting of today's ethnic slurs. Nor were our neighbors insulted by stereotypes. One's heritage did not matter. People accepted you for what you were. Contact, not media imagery, shaped personal relationships.

My memories of the past, when people were looked upon as individuals—and current stereotypes, that paint ethnic groups with a broad brush—led me to write about the portrayal of Arabs on TV. Ethnic stereotypes and caricatures corrupt the imagination, narrow our vision and blur reality. My hope in writing this book is to eventually see a more balanced view of Arabs on television: to find in Arab television characters the equivalent of my mother, Nazara, and my grandparents, Jacob and Naffa, people who had compassion for *all* other peoples. This work is also for my children and others, so as they grow up, they will experience the joy of accepting people as they are.

In Search of the Arabs

This book reflects man's quest for fair play, not for a single group of misunderstood and seriously misrepresented human beings, but for all men and women, of all ethnic and religious backgrounds, everywhere.

I base this work in part on eight years of television viewing. Beginning with the 1975-76 TV season, I have documented over 100 different popular entertainment programs, cartoons and major documentaries telecast on network, independent and public channels, totaling nearly 200 episodes, that relate to Arabs.

Turn to any channel, to any show from *Benson* to *Hart to Hart* television is full of Arab baddies—billionaires, bombers and belly dancers. They are virtually the only TV images of Arabs viewers ever see. An episode of a popular entertainment program may be seen by 40 million people the first time it is telecast. With reruns, the program may attract a total of 150 million viewers.

Television tends to perpetuate four basic myths about Arabs: they are all fabulously wealthy; they are barbaric and uncultured; they are sex maniacs with a penchant for white slavery; and they revel in acts of terrorism. Yet, just a little surface probing reveals that these notions are as false as the assertions that Blacks are lazy, Hispanics are dirty, Jews are greedy and Italians are criminals:

After all, like every national or ethnic group, Arabs are made up of **good** decent people, with the usual mix of one-percenters, the bad **apples** found in any barrel.

Television executives permit the stereotype because they do not know much about Arabs on their nations. Nor have they taken the time to find out, a conclusion sadly arrived at after personally conducting extensive interviews with the men and women who decide what will be seen on TV.

The image can best be described as "The Instant TV Arab Kit." The kit, suitable for most TV Arabs, consists of a belly dancer's outfit, headdresses (which look like tablecloths pinched from a restaurant), veils, sunglasses, flowing gowns and robes, oil wells, limousines and/or camels. Those rare occasions when a program attempted to reveal fair observations of Arab life, past or present, were more than offset by television shows and movies with the all-too-familiar stereotypes. Hollywood films preserve traditional stereotypes and television shows follow Hollywood's lead. The result is that the TV Arab becomes a rerun of a rerun.

This odious phenomenon, the stereotype, is defined as "a standardized conception or image invested with special meaning." But more often than not, the stereotype has other connotations attributed to groups of people, portraying them as persona non grata.

In Los Angeles, Harve Bennett, producer of the *Six Million Dollar Man* and the *Bionic Woman* told me: "I don't have any explanation for stereotyping other than it's easy. Let me put it this way—do you know how to play charades? Television is one great charade," said Bennett. "You don't go for the meat of the material. You do a pantomime of a guy in a burnoose. But it's sign language and that's the trouble. That's the temptation. Put him in a burnoose and we'll all know who he is."

The producer said stereotyping saves the writer "the ultimate discomfort of having to think." But he noted that the medium itself sometimes forces the writer to give characters and subjects only cursory treatment. "Sometimes, unthinkingly, and under pressure of getting material out in a medium that has no lead time, everybody tends to think in terms of quick solutions. I think the tendency to target Arabs for fun and anger is very easy and is often done," Bennett said.

My stereotyping project began as a solo effort to analyze programs, but members of my family, friends and colleagues assisted by calling my attention to dramas I might otherwise have missed. Sometimes, when visiting friends, conversations over dinner would stop at a certain point and someone would say they had seen another TV Arab. If nothing else, they were becoming sensitive to the fact that the negative portrayal of Arabs is as serious as stereotyping of Orientals, Native Americans and other groups.

For years I watched hordes of TV Arabs parade across the screen. It was a disturbing experience, similar to walking into those mirrored rooms at amusement parks where all you see is distorted self-images. To go beyond personal observations, I decided to seek out those responsible for the degrading caricatures. In the summer and fall of 1980 I arranged to interview more than thirty people directly involved with creating the television images of various ethnic groups. I met with broadcast standards executives in Los Angeles, New York and Washington, at ABC, NBC and CBS. (CBS labels its broadcast standards office "program practices department.") I also met with writers and producers of entertainment shows and documentaries.

Some producers and writers told me that broadcast standards executives, sometimes referred to as network "censors," have a limited influence on what is on the screen. Others say they can and do affect program content. I believe programming responsibility rests with network executives as well as producers and writers—the creators of television programs. Unlike network "censors" who offer guidelines, producers and writers spawn the ideas, formats and cast of characters. Their decisions usually determine the success or failure of given programs.

While transcribing the tapes of the interviews, alone in my study, I reflected on the attitudes and responses of those who had met with me. I recalled that some people were openly prejudiced, others misguided or misinformed. A majority, however, seemed to be honest, sincere and intelligent men and women who truly want to serve their viewers well. At ABC in Los Angeles, for example, broadcast standards Vice President Tom Kersey made special arrangements for me to meet with his staff. Kersey and his associate, Don Bay, said they believe in bringing "intelligence to the table." They were receptive and anxious to know more details about "real" Arabs. After discussions with ABC's staff members, one of them, a Mexican-American, took me aside and whispered, "I feel your pain."

In Los Angeles, I also spoke with Jerome Stanley, NBC's vice president for broadcast standards. I asked him why Arabs are "fair game." Stanley replied, "I don't think one can point the finger at television and television alone. Television entertainment producers, like news reporters, sometimes take their information from newspaper headlines, editorial cartoons and articles in magazines rather than generate the information themselves."

"I think some of the superficial stories that we have seen in other media just kind of filter down to network producers," he continued. "That information, although we would like to think otherwise, becomes a part of one's philosophy and is accepted and used when working with programs."

I chose the television medium because it is a predominant source and distributor of popular culture. U.S. population now exceeds 225 million, and ninety-eight percent of all households have at least one TV set; most sets are turned on a minimum of six and a half hours every day. Ninety million Americans watch nightly prime time shows.

According to Dr. George Gerbner, Dean of the Annenberg School of Communications at the University of Pennsylvania, "Television more than any single institution molds American behavioral norms and values. And the more TV we watch," Dr. Gerbner maintains, "the more we tend to believe in the world according to TV, even though much of what we see is misleading."

Television possesses the greatest potential for promoting better understanding among peoples of the world. As the leading exporter of television programs, America transmits lifestyles and perceptions of ethnic groups far beyond its borders—to viewers in Africa, Asia, Australia, Europe, the Middle East and South America. As the leader, we have responsibilities to fulfill.

How well are we fulfilling them? In 1980, researcher Shelley Slade cited a poll among average Americans to see how they perceive Arabs. Answers such as "anti-American," "anti-Christian," "cunning," "unfriendly" and "warlike" were common. Slade's research, published later in *The Middle East Journal*, also revealed that Americans have scant knowledge of Arab accomplishments.

This ignorance becomes self-perpetuating. Meg Greenfield, editorial page editor of *The Washington Post*, has said that we misunderstand the Arabs and this results in "an Arab caricature." Greenfield believes, "There is a dehumanizing, circular process at work here. The caricature dehumanizes." But the caricature "is inspired and made acceptable by an earlier dehumanizing influence, namely an absence of feeling for who the Arabs are and where they have been," she writes.

When I think of the word "Arab," I see the 150 million people in the great expanse of the Arab world, most of whom share a common cultural heritage, religion and history.

They are city dwellers, suburbanites, farmers and villagers who live in twenty-one different countries. Many wear Western-styled dresses, trousers, shirts, ties and coats. Some Arab men cover their heads with a small embroidered or crocheted cap, over which they place the traditional *kufiyah*, a white or checkered cloth which is folded diagonally and kept in place by two rings of thick black wool called the *agal*. Some Arab women go veiled in the streets or wear just head scarves of smoke-thin chiffon or opaque black crepe. Other women wear the latest fashions from Paris and London and New York. Still others wear the traditional *abaya* (chiffon gowns). The variety of white, brown and black-skinned Arab men, women and children defies stereotyping.

Very little is known in the U.S. about outstanding Arab personalities. Thanks to Sir Walter Scott's novel, *The Talisman*, some of us know about the 12th century Arab champion of chivalry, Saladin, who defeated Richard the Lionhearted and conquered Jerusalem from the Crusaders. This remarkable warrior carried with him the traditions of Arab warfare, which prohibited the killing of the elderly, women and children. Saladin, whose name means the "bounty of religion," did not persecute the defeated Christians but permitted them to continue to live in peace with Moslems in the holy city.

Another giant of Arab culture, the contemporary Lebanese poet, philosopher and artist, Kahlil Gibran, spent most of his life in the United States writing about love, religion and freedom. Of Gibran's numerous books, his most popular poetic work, *The Prophet*, appears in more than twenty languages. Approximately a quarter of a million copies are sold each year in the United States.

Creators of TV programs could easily offer viewers significant programs about past and present Arab personalities like Saladin and Gibran. There are also contemporary heroes, like Egypt's Um Kalthoum, a peasant girl who became one of the world's richest and most famous women. As a renowned singer, she regularly performed special concerts for Egypt's needy. For fifty years her songs of love appealed to the hearts and minds of Arabs. She could sing for five consecutive hours without stopping. When she died in 1975, the Egyptian government did not release the news for seven days, fearing public chaos. The media transmitted daily reports about her "illness." Until now, no single death has been so mourned by the Arab people.

Another contemporary hero is Huda Sharawi, also of Egypt and a pioneer of the Arab Women's Liberation Movement, who led several demonstrations in her country in the early part of the century against the oppression of women and the British occupation. A promoter of national independence, she was known as the "Mother of the Modern Egyptian Family." Ms. Sharawi wrote for and established political pamphlets and magazines in French and Arabic which supported women's rights. She also advocated the abolishment of prostitution and warned against atomic armaments.

There is also Lebanese-born Rose Elyousef, an actress and famous journalist/publisher, who performed on stage in the early 1900s when women were generally forbidden to appear in dramas. In Egypt, she established a weekly arts magazine, *Rose Elyousef*, which helped defend her and other actresses against public criticism. The magazine, the first to employ women as journalists, encountered ruthless opposition from officials. In another courageous move, Elyousef changed the content of *Rose Elyousef* from art to politics. Again, the authorities harassed her and other staff members by censoring and periodically closing the magazine. Yet, she not only continued publishing *Rose Elyousef* but established a major publishing house. After Elyousef's death in 1944, her daughter Fatima started another famous weekly magazine, *Sabah El Kheir (Good Morning)*. Both publications are known for their cartoons and sketches instead of photographs and remain available on today's newsstands. Her son, Ishan Abd Quodoos, who acts as editor-in-chief of both magazines, is also one of the Arab world's best novelists.

Television programs also generally ignore Arab contributions to world civilization. The Arabs gave the world a religion—Islam—a language and an alphabet. Between the 9th and 12th centuries, a number of Arab scholars wrote important documents on medicine, philosophy, history, religion, astronomy and geography. Hundreds of English words we use today are a sign of this legacy: algebra, zero, cipher, alcohol. The list runs on. Many of the original Arabic manuscripts were later translated and used in European schools. Famous Arab surgeons in the Middle Ages authored books and medical encyclopedias that, in Latin translation, became leading medical texts in European universities.

Arab doctors made numerous breakthroughs in the areas of drugs and surgery and wrote extensively on diseases and treatments. They were pioneers in introducing the kind of teaching hospitals and traveling clinics which served as models for Western countries. Arabs were the first to establish hospitals with different wards for different diseases and to restrict the practice of medicine to medical college graduates with diplomas. In surgery, they were the first to perform the procedure we know today as the caesarean section.

Arab physicians, who discovered the contagious nature of tuberculosis, recognized the highly infectious nature of the plague. They demonstrated that the disease could be transmitted by clothing and utensils as well as by personal contact. They were the first to diagnose stomach cancer, measles, smallpox, cholera and bubonic plague. All this occurred 300 years before Pasteur's bacteriological discoveries.

Arab scholars adapted Hindu numerals into the numbers system we still use in a modified form today, invented algebra, made revolutionary advances in geometry and trigonometry and taught the use of ciphers.

In astronomy, Arabs established the use of latitude and longitude. They built the world's first observatory in western Iraq. When the telescope was still unknown, Arabs made important contributions in the use of observational instruments such as astrolabes, star maps and celestial globes. They introduced the concept of the center of gravity and prescribed to the ancient Greek theory that the world is round before Columbus ultimately proved it.

In Europe, Islamic contributions are of an everlasting value. The Arabs from North Africa focused on southern Spain, what they called al-Andalus (Andalusia), and built a remarkable civilization there. Moslem Arabs treated Christians and Jews with tolerance, so that many of them embraced Islam. Arabs established Cordoba as the most sophisticated city in Europe. By the 10th century Cordoba boasted a population of nearly 500,000, compared to about 38,000 in Paris. The city had 700 mosques, some 900 public baths, Europe's first street lights, a water and sewage system, libraries, hospitals and research institutions.

One of Cordoba's scholars was Abbas Ibn-Firnas, who constructed a pair of wings out of feathers on a wooden frame and made the first attempt to fly, anticipating Leonardo da Vinci by some 600 years. He also designed a planetarium. Not only was it mechanized—the planets actually rotated—but it simulated thunder and lightning. In 1154 the famous Cordoban scientist and poet al-Idrisi wrote a systematic geography of the world known as the *Book of Roger*, after his patron Roger II, the Norman King of Sicily. Arab geographers understood the basic outlines of Asia, North Africa and Europe by the 12th century, and their knowledge was documented in al-Idrisi's impressive atlas.

The greatest geographer of Africa was an Arab, Hassan al-Wazzan. In the 16th century the Church brought him before Pope Leo X to write an account of his African travels. In time, al-Wazzan's work appeared in many languages and for over 200 years served as the most authoritative account of Africa. Another Arab, Yaqut Ibn Abdullah al-Hamawi, wrote a geographical dictionary considered to be a forerunner to the modern-day encyclopedia. Important thinkers who flourished in the West in the 13th century, such as Roger Bacon, John Duns Scotus and St. Albert the Great, acknowledged their debts to Arab scholars.

In the field of optics, Ibn al-Haytham made scientific progress with studies on focusing, magnifying, inversion of the image and the formation of rings and colors. His works helped influence Roger Bacon and Leonardo da Vinci, among others.

The Arabs invented the clock. Some of their time pieces moved by water, others by mercury or burning candles. The most famous is the water clock given to Charlemagne of France in 807 by the caliph

Haroun al-Rashid.

They contributed to music theory, being the first to give time values to specific tones. The guitar and lute were originally Arab instruments. Arab architecture inspired the Gothic style and the Crusaders learned how to build fortifications from their Arab antagonists. The Arabs were pioneers in water works, a major preoccupation of people who live in arid or semi-arid lands. As technicians, they built dams, used water wheels, dug wells, irrigation systems and underground canals. In agriculture, they introduced oranges, the cotton shrub, the mulberry bush, sugar cane and date palms.

Like other people, Arabs have made many contributions to civilization. Yet these contributions are rarely shown on our television screens.

Part of the problem of correcting TV images stems from television's need for universal villains. The villain of choice today is the Arab. Because we face rising gas prices, oil-fueled inflation and tough competition from other nations, some of them our former enemies, we always seem to need someone to kick around.

As columnist Russell Baker points out in a *New York Times* article, "Pillowed in Araby," we usually blame someone else for our problems. Baker underscored his point in this satiric conversation between buyer and seller:

> "This apartment is only $250,000."
> "Isn't that a little steep?"
> "It's the Arabs."

In *The American Media and the Arabs*, ABC newsman Steve Bell says the choice of a villain in drama is "dependent to a great degree on the headline events that attract public interest, and the 'villain of the hour' in America has changed frequently." Bell points out how at one time the Chinese communists were seen as Enemy Number One, intent on controlling the world and capable of calling on hordes of mindless zealots to overwhelm the forces of freedom with their very mass. All of this, says Bell, "was very much based on current events and the concern of the American public about the Chinese role and potential in those events. The Nixon trip to Peking changed all that."

To coincide with President Nixon's visit, CBS produced a documentary, *Misunderstanding China*. The film documented Chinese stereotypes in motion pictures and implied that Fu Manchu images had been so widely accepted only because of politics and ignorance of Chinese culture. Our government's diplomatic recognition of China soon changed the perceptions of China for the better.

Likewise, the civil rights movement of the 1960s did much to curb the Stepin-Fetchet-type portrayal of blacks on television. The movement also helped bring to the screen a more realistic, human portrayal of Hispanics and American Indians. Some old movies and TV reruns continue to stereotype blacks and other minorities. But nowadays blacks appear as doctors, lawyers and scientists in television dramas, and not just as janitors and domestics, though not in numbers comparable to those in real life. Once banned from television commercials, blacks now appear as "typical" American families who worry over what toothpaste to use, what brand of cereal to eat. Hispanics are no longer Mexican banditos. Rarely are Indians portrayed anymore as screaming tribes who massacre helpless whites. The Oriental is no longer a shuffling coolie or sadistic, slanty-eyed villain. Television has done well to abandon pejorative characterizations of these minorities. However, the Arab has not received the same "second look" from the media as have other groups. And Americans continue to know very little about real-life Arabs.

As defined in the 1947 edition of Webster's New International Dictionary, "The Arabs are one of the oldest and purest of peoples, and with the Jews, constitute the best modern representatives of the Semitic race."

The present-day Arab stereotype parallels the image of Jews in pre-Nazi Germany, where Jews were painted as dark, shifty-eyed, venal and threateningly different people. After the holocaust, the characterization of Jews as murderous anarchists or greedy financiers was no longer tolerable. Many cartoonists, however, reincarnated this caricature and transferred it to another group of Semites, the Arabs. Only now it wears a robe and a headdress instead of a yarmulke and a Star of David.

Ben Hecht, the noted writer, was provoked to comment: "Anti-Semitism is an easy trick even for the most amateur of villains. It is more than a trick. It is an oasis in which saints can disport themselves lecherously, a little ward of lunacy in which philosophers can relax, and a prescription for the cure of acne, frostbite, ulcers, and many other diseases." Hecht's words, though written in the early 1940s, apply to both Arabs and Jews.

Years ago, the Anti-Defamation League of B'nai B'rith succeeded in stopping a great deal of overt anti-Jewish slander. In the early 1900s, organizers of the League were faced with a deluge of "motion pictures that mercilessly ridiculed the Jew, his religion and his culture." The League believes that when one ethnic or racial group is attacked, all groups suffer.

The Arab stereotype has been part of our culture ever since cameras started cranking. Motion pictures of the early 1900s presented Arabia as an exotic land, with harems and seductive belly dancers. Many of today's perceptions can be traced to *the* motion picture of the 1920s, *The Sheik*, starring Rudolph Valentino. The film spurred the practice of lumping Arabs—Egyptians, Iraqis, Lebanese, Bahrainis and others—as a collective group. The film also spawned the illusion of the romantic sheik who abducts young ladies and confines them in his desert tent. Valentino's character turns out to be, despite his burnoose and desert tan, none other than a Scottish earl, who had been abandoned in the Sahara as a baby. A Scotsman, not an Arab, turns out to be the great lover and seducer of English ladies.

Television has replaced the movie's seductive sheik of the 1920s with the hedonistic oil sheik of the 1980s. In today's films and television shows, Arabs do not only pursue women, but a host of things, like American real estate, businesses and government officials.

"The great enemy of truth is very often not the lie—deliberate, continued and dishonest—but the myth, persistent, persuasive and unrealistic," said President John F. Kennedy. TV writers employ many myths about Arabs. Here are some of them.

ARABS ARE BUYING UP AMERICA. The Arab is hardly in the financial picture except on television. In reality, almost ninety percent of direct foreign investment in the U.S. during 1980 was accounted for by the Netherlands, the United Kingdom, Canada, Germany, the Netherlands Antilles, Japan, Switzerland and France. "The members of the OPEC together accounted for less than one percent of the total," according to U.S. Department of Commerce reports.

Only three percent of U.S. farm land changes hands each year and Arabs buy only .0015 percent of the agricultural land sold annually. Arab investors are no different from other investors—Israelis, Australians, British. They value the U.S. for its diverse market, political stability and free enterprise, notes economic and political analyst John Law in his book, *Arab Investors: Who They Are, What They Buy and Where*. Law writes, "Arab investment, in the broad sense of the term, is hardly new. Arabs have been investing for thousands of years, just as other people have."

Law says that Arab investors do not act as a group. Governments, companies and individuals are investing here. "But there is no such thing," says Law, "as an OPEC investment policy in the United States, however often this has been held up as a chimera by Congressional committees. OPEC countries, including the Arab ones, go their own ways. So do individual Arab investors, who, far from launching any conspiracy to buy up America or Europe, tend to be as competitive abroad as they are at home."

Arab investors as a whole, says Law, "are extremely sensitive to any hostile situations in the countries in which they invest." He explains that a banker who is one of the wealthiest men in Saudi Arabia, turned down an opportunity to buy a major U.S. company badly in need of capital, because of the repercussions he feared would result when the public learned that a product with a famous name had become "Arab property."

Too much is also made of Arab wealth. In 1979 Libya and the wealthier oil-producing countries of the Arabian Gulf—Saudi Arabia, Qatar, Kuwait and the United Arab Emirates—had an average per capita income of slightly more than $12,000. (U.S. per capita income in 1979 was $10,600). According to a 1981 World Bank Development Report, the other Arab cultures had a per capita income of less than $850 per year.

OPEC IS SYNONYMOUS WITH ARAB. For many Americans, the acronym OPEC means Arab with a negative connotation, but in reality only about half of OPEC's members are Arab nations. Yet, on television and in the public eye, the Organization of Petroleum Exporting Countries (OPEC) has become synonymous with Arab. At a California convention in 1982, the Chrysler Corporation's chairman of the board, Lee Iacocca, proposed that a tax be levied on all imported oil. Said Iacocca, "Kick the Arabs while they're down—that's what we should be doing." Iacocca perpetuates the myth that most U.S. oil imports come from Arab nations. In fact, "The United States obtains only about 5 percent of its imported oil from the (Arabian) Gulf. Saudi Arabia (is in) sixth place, behind Mexico, Canada, Venezuela, Britain and Indonesia" (*Newsweek,* March 12, 1984, p. 12). Some television commercials also play upon national frustrations by citing OPEC members as the culprits that cause inflation. Mr. Iacocca appealed to the patriotic spirit of viewers when he declared in a Chrysler commercial, "If everyone in America drove a K-car (a Chrysler economy car), we wouldn't have to import a single drop of OPEC oil." The Chrysler commercials feature Yankee Doodle music and a celebrity—Angie Dickinson, Gregory Peck, George Kennedy or Frank Sinatra—who announce "America is not going to be pushed around any more." The TV ads are really asking: What will it be, America, a red-white-and-blue K-car, or bowing to OPEC crude? Television critic Judith Hennessee contends that Chrysler's spots "hark back to those glorious days when we could send in the Marines and have done with it."

When TV anchors say "OPEC," viewers often see a bearded, robed Arab appear on the screen. But the fact remains that only seven of the thirteen OPEC members are Arab nations. Of the five largest oil-producing nations, only one, Saudi Arabia, is Arab. The Saudis are OPEC's most moderate member, usually voting against exorbitant price increases. They increased oil production in 1978 through 1980 at a price four dollars per barrel below that of other major producers. In contrast, the role of the U.S. oil companies in price-setting rarely receives mention in television newscasts.

IRANIANS ARE ARABS. No, Iranians are Persians. They are not Semites, as Arabs are. But nearly everyone I interviewed thought Iranians are Arabs. Iranians are primarily Aryans who moved onto the Persian plateau in the 17th century B.C. Persia was renamed Iran in the 1930s when the former Shah Reza Pahlavi's family seized power. Iranians do not speak Arabic, they speak Farsi, an Indo-European tongue that shares several common characteristics with Western European languages.

ALL ARABS ARE MOSLEMS. A host of simple-minded cliches about Moslems and Islam exists. When the hostage crisis in Iran occurred, most Westerners began to view all Moslems, the followers of Islam, as Arab or Iranian militants seeking to return the world to the 14th century. There is, however, great diversity in Islam, a religion that covers one-seventh of the earth's inhabitable area and includes a sixth of its population. To judge all Moslems as the same is as futile as judging all Christians and Jews in the same way. Most of the world's 800 million Moslems are not fatalistic radicals. Like most Christians and Jews, they, too, devoutly believe in and respect God and seek to live a good life in peace with others.

Many educated people confuse the Arab world with the Moslem world. Geographically, Arab countries stretch along Northern Africa and into the Middle East. But the Moslem world overlaps the Arab world and stretches far beyond to most of Africa continuing eastward through India, Indonesia and the Philippines. Not all of the Arab world's 150 million people are Moslem, though many, of course, are both.

Former news correspondent, radio announcer and author, Edward J. Byng, writes in his book *The World of the Arabs*, "Our Western picture of Islam and of the Arabs is a pitiful caricature of the reality. It is the result of thirteen hundred years of religious propaganda." In Arabic, "Islam" means submission to God. A religion that celebrated its 1400th anniversary in 1981, Islam provides an all-inclusive system for social and religious conduct based upon the Koran (divine revelations) and the teachings of the prophet Mohammed. It is monotheistic and shares values and traditions with Christianity and Judaism. For example, Abraham (Ibrahim, in Arabic) is considered by Moslems as the father of all monotheistic people and is thus revered in Islam. Mohammed is the *last* prophet, following the footsteps of Abraham, Moses and Jesus. Islam's most basic acts of faith are usually called "The Five Pillars of Islam"—Profession of Faith, Prayer, Almsgiving, Fasting and Pilgrimage.

But on TV entertainment programs, when performers refer to "Allah" or Islam, viewers do not see devout worshippers. TV often shows Islam as a religion that permits a man to have many wives and concubines and condones beheadings and stoning people to death. Although "Allah" means God, when performers say "Allah" on TV it is usually with the intent of evoking laughter, cynicism, or the image of some vaguely pagan deity.

ARABS ARE WHITE SLAVERS AND UNCIVILIZED RULERS OF KINGDOMS. Many writers portray the Arab as one who kidnaps young Americans and then sentences them to a "fate worse than death" as slaves. There are no slave markets today in the Middle East.

The popular conception of Arabs as slavers started in the 19th century with some European explorers and missionaries. One man, who made allegations to the British public about Arabs as slavers, was the famous missionary teacher and philanthropist, David Livingstone.

Professor Sari Nasir, of the University of Jordan, says that Livingstone failed to gain converts to Christianity in Africa. The Scottish missionary-teacher also suggested that "the Arabs must be forced out of Africa and replaced by Christian missionaries, in order to redeem the continent." Nasir points out, ironically, that slavery and slave trade existed in Britain until the early 19th century. As the world became more "civilized," slavery was abolished in Europe, the United States and in the Middle East.

ALL PALESTINIANS ARE TERRORISTS. The TV image fails to reflect the true diversity of 4.4 million Palestinians who mostly live as exiles, scattered throughout the Middle East and beyond. During three decades of dispersal Palestinians have developed an intense sense of community. They yearn to once again have a home they can call their own.

The stereotype obscures the peaceable Palestinian multitude—those men and women who work as diplomats, doctors, professors, artists, farmers, engineers, shopkeepers and homemakers.

Former President Jimmy Carter has said that any permanent solution to the Arab-Israeli conflict would require Israel "to honor Palestinian rights." Carter explained, "I see hundreds of thousands of

Palestinians deprived of a home, deprived of a right to own property, deprived of a right to assemble, deprived of a right of free speech, deprived of a right to vote and...approaching a generation under military rule.... This is not only contrary to established world custom, but it's also directly in violation of the heritage of the Jews and it is anomalous in an Israeli nation."

Viewers mainly see Palestinians as an evil mass of masked faces. This slanted view persists in spite of some balanced documentaries, newscasts, magazine and newspaper reports about the Palestinian people which show that most of them want peace.

Time magazine's cover story, "Children of War," of January 11, 1982, takes a look at thirty children from five war-torn nations. Senior writer Roger Rosenblatt gives an intensely personal account of how the children—Palestinian and Israeli—view life when it might explode before their eyes at any moment. Rosenblatt downplays stereotypes and concentrates instead on the human suffering of both sides. He fairly documents terrorist actions by both parties—Israelis killed by Palestinian-launched rockets and Palestinians killed by Israeli bombs.

The Palestinian people merely seek an identity: their own flag, land and country, where they can make their own decisions and elect their own leaders. One Palestinian youth says to author Grace Halsell, in her book *Journey to Jerusalem*, that he wants "the American freedom to travel, to borrow money, and to find a part-time job while pursuing a career. These are realities millions of Americans take for granted. But to a man without a country and without a passport, they are miracles."

An American woman once remarked to a friend of mine, "I don't know which jolts people more: to say my child is autistic or to say my husband is Palestinian." A Palestinian-American woman I know, who owns a public relations firm, tells people she is Italian for fear she will lose both friends and clients if they discover her Palestinian heritage.

INTRA-ARAB STRIFE. The Arab family is often self-destructive. Writers for *Casablanca, The Rockford Files,* the *Bionic Woman* and other shows portray the Arab woman as dominated by men. Backward and confined by the harem, she usually submits to her master's wishes, but her susbservient charm seldom attracts the master. The progressive Arab woman, as TV would have it, is often too good for the Arab male. Her liberal behavior sometimes results in a death sentence pronounced by members of her own family. Father and brothers appear as uncivilized men with mute bodyguards. The sons fight each other to gain control of the father's kingdom.

In reality, close family ties prevail throughout the Middle East. When I first visited Lebanon, with my wife and two children, in 1974, we were welcomed by an administrator from the American University of Beirut—plus five carloads of our relatives. It is customary for families to greet guests with such fanfare. And after a 27-hour flight we shared mixed emotions—excitement and confusion.

A tug-of-war immediately ensued, followed by whispers and private consultations. Our cousins insisted we go with them to Hamate, the village of my parents. The university administrator demanded we stay at a nearby hotel. Cousin Rudolph settled the dispute: he grabbed us and the luggage. Off we went, chugging along in a VW bus held together by Arab ingenuity.

The first night in Hamate was uneventful. We could not sleep. Nor could we communicate. And I was a professor of communications. Their broken English and our broken Arabic centered only on food.

Breakfast that first morning was a 30-course meal: fresh meat, fish and vegetables plus Arab sweets, coffee and tea—breakfast, lunch and dinner all at one sitting. My cousins are typical. Giving of themselves to others, especially family, is part of their tradition. In Hamate, married couples live with or near their parents—by choice. Streets are safe. Educated youngsters speak a minimum of two languages.

Shortly after I arrived in Hamate, I received a cable from Pennsylvania stating my Aunt Ann had passed away. In Hamate, I shared tears with Ann's sister, my Aunt Munera. Although they lived thousands of miles apart and had spent little time together in recent years, they remained close. At the local Eastern Orthodox church in Hamate, nearly the entire village attended the memorial mass for Ann.

During quiet moments, I remember the sorrow and joy of the stay there. I remember the wedding we attended where musicians came to the village carrying home-made drums and flutes fastened to dark, worn goat skins. Hundreds of people joined hands and danced the *Dubkeh* (an Arab folk dance). We sang songs, ate freshly-picked fruits, nuts and fresh roasted chicken with rice and raisins, meat and spinach pies, and baked eggplant. A few boasting souls, such as myself, drank too much *Arak* (a strong liquor with anise flavor) until sunrise. Both the wedding and memorial mass reflect what we do not see on television screens— Arab roots, Arab feelings of family, of life and death.

ARABS ARE THE WORLD'S ENEMIES. The record proves otherwise. Saudi Arabia is one of the world's largest aid donors. Saudi Prince Talal Ibn Abdul Aziz is a dedicated fundraiser for UNICEF; yet, on TV, Arabs are seen as irresponsible spenders. Viewers suspect foul play when a TV program shows an Arab working on a business deal with an American. We see few scenes of Arab-American business ventures based on friendships. Who would ever suspect that there are forty-seven Arab Rotary Clubs, nineteen in Egypt alone? There are sixty-eight Arab Lion's Clubs—twenty-four of which are in Lebanon. These Arab businessmen, whether educated at home or abroad, know that good business is based on trust, on planning and on offering high quality products and services.

Official U.S. government policy is positive about foreign investment "from all countries." Such investments provide "benefits to the U.S. economy, such as increased employment, new technology, and new production and managerial techniques," says Robert A. Cornell, Deputy Assistant Secretary for Trade and Investment Policy.

In October, 1983, Treasury Secretary Donald Regan met with Arab officials in Saudi Arabia, Kuwait and Bahrain, said Cornell. The Secretary raised the issue of Arab investments in the U.S.—and the fact that the U.S. would like more of them. He cited Secretary Regan's emphasis that "the free flow of foreign investment fosters economic efficiency and thereby benefits both home and host countries and the world economy."

Television programs ignore the fact that Arab-American partnerships benefit both sides. One example of a Saudi-American business venture is Saudi Arabia's multi-billion dollar gas-gathering project—which calls for the use of more than 100 compressors. The Saudis are paying approximately $60 million for the compressors, machined and assembled in the U.S. Over half the compressors are being produced by a small firm in Jeanette, Pennsylvania, the Elliot Company.

"Saudi Arabia has developed into a major trading partner with the United States," said Karl S. Reiner of the U.S. Department of Commerce. Reiner points out in an issue of *Saudi Business* that exports from the United States to Saudi Arabia reached $5.7 billion in 1980. The projected exports in 1981 were $6.5 billion.

"No other country in modern times has advanced so far so quickly," said *Time* correspondent James Kelly. Saudi Arabia is the largest U.S. market in the Middle East—the sixth largest among America's top trade partners around the world. Approximately 40,000 Americans work in Saudi Arabia; there are over 500 U.S. firms; many of them help construct mini-cities for construction workers. Holmes & Narver, Inc., of Nevada has worked on twenty-seven mini-cities so far. Each city will accommodate 4,000 to 10,000 workers and will have recreational facilties, including swimming pools. Some $130 million in supplies have been ordered from various states, and that is only a small part of the project. For example, 441 poolside lounge chairs will come from Tennessee; 9,000 complete sets of dinnerware from Pennsylvania; 1,760 bunk beds from New York; and 4,416 bath towels from North Carolina.

The Arab world will number 300 million people by the year 2000. Its natural settings of rolling deserts, forested mountains, white beaches and lush green river banks are ripe for the cinematographer's lens. There are untold stories to be heard within Arab communities. The emerging conflicts of individuals building nations while attempting to maintain valued religious and social traditions are many. Will their nations become so "modern" that social unity and faith decline? Will Arab folklore and language continue to survive alongside innovative ideas? Or will the technological future mute the Arab traditions of humor, poetry and song? Will the educated young, those who have studied at Arab universities or in Europe and the United States, continue to care for their parents at home? Or will they feel this is the responsibility of the state, of institutions? Will Western dress, already an accepted style in most Arab countries, reflect an actual change in social roles and attitudes?

The drama of the Arab world awaits the television artist. But in order to capture such drama, the artist must first have a sincere motivation to care and to perceive. The artist might better follow those guidelines established by the Anti-Defamation League of the B'nai B'rith and "put an end forever to unjust and unfair discrimination against and ridicule of any sect or body of citizens."

Most perceptions of Arabs today come not from real knowledge but from faulty and simplistic assumptions. The writer and producer, in cooperation with broadcast standards officials, will convey a truer image when they begin to *see* Arabs—indeed all people—as the multi-faceted beings they are.

Children and Teens

Television quite possibly has its strongest impact on small children. They are quickly captivated by its images and quickly absorb the notions of life that the medium serves up for better or for worse.

Even before children begin school, they watch more than 30 hours a week of television. Most young adults spend at least a fifth of their waking hours in front of the set, says David Pearl, chief of the National Institute of Mental Health's Behavioral Sciences Research Bureau. By the time a youngster completes high school, he will have spent twice as many hours watching television as he spent in the classrooms—22,000 hours of accumulated viewing time before the TV screen and only 11,000 hours of classroom time.

Children are not born with prejudice against races or religious groups. Carlos Cortes, Professor of History and Chairman of Chicano Studies at the University of California at Riverside, points out that before many children reach school they will have developed well-formed attitudes about ethnic groups, "including prejudices and stereotypes." Cortes believes television has a particularly powerful impact, "often outweighing personal experience." In the April 1979 issue of *Journal of Educational Leadership,* he cites a survey that found that fourth, eighth and twelfth graders formed attitudes about foreign nations and peoples largely on what they learned of them through television, which unfortunately frequently stereotypes.

"Cultural stereotyping deprives minorities of respect," Cortes says. He adds that stereotypes are illogical, but once formed they tend to persist, even in the face of contradictory evidence and experience. For example, a friend who teaches high school students in Detroit, Michigan, told me about an incident in which his twelfth graders became angry with him when he challenged television's portrayal of Arabs as the perennial bad guys. The television image was so *real* to the

21

students that they vigorously protested when presented with evidence that countered the Arab stereotype.

"Stereotypes are not based upon valid experience," notes Professor Elliot Aronson, who teaches psychology at the University of California in Santa Cruz. In his book, *The Social Animal*, Professor Aronson points out that stereotypes "are based on hearsay or images concocted by the mass media, or are generated within our heads as ways of justifying our own prejudices and cruelty."

Testifying before a 1980 hearing of the House Select Committee on Aging, actress Janet MacLachlan expressed concern about television stereotyping, especially in children's programs. She described her ten-year-old-daughter as a "TV junkie" who receives most of her information about the world from that outlet. "Her attitudes about people," said MacLachlan, "the relationship between them and about herself are skewed by the medium—by the unrealistic and stereotyped portrayals of the elderly, of black people, of Asian, Latin-Hispanic, American Indian people." As a result, MacLachlan said, "the child equates age with tragedy, and skin color with negativity and failure." Through television's fantasies, countless viewers "act out their subliminal fears and prejudices," MacLachlan said. "The decision-makers responsible for television programming refuse to acknowledge that the medium they control has the power to influence all our attitudes and expectations . . . . 'It's just entertainment,' they say; 'we're only giving our audiences what the ratings show they want'."

Arabs are certainly not the only group whose children are affected by the negative stereotypes that pour from television's cornucopia of nonsense. In the late 1960s, black entertainers expressed concern about TV's effect on black children in big-city ghettos. Bill Cosby, the first positive black male in a TV series, said that these youths had too few black heroes they could pattern their lives after. As a result, said Cosby, they idolized dope peddlers and pimps who drove flashy cars and found ways to beat the system. Diahann Carroll echoed Cosby's sentiments: "It is important that Negro children have symbols with which they can identify." Miss Carroll added that television should help children become proud of their blackness.

In Los Angeles, ABC's Vice President of Broadcast Standards and Practices, Tom Kersey, spoke with me about meeting several years ago with cartoonists Hanna and Barbera "to find an identifiably black hero to bring to television." Said Kersey, "We searched this town, we searched Chicago, we searched New York for a proper cartoon." They eventually came up with a Black Vulcan character. "One of the most sincere promises this department can make is the inclusion of minorities in positive portrayals in all of our programming," said Kersey.

Today Arab-American youngsters must search hard to find an Arab role model on television. Their parents may try to instill in them ethnic pride, but television bombards them with negative Arab images. Sometimes this experience carries over into the classroom. For example, the hostage situation in Iran caused many Americans to confuse Iranians with Arabs. During this crisis, some children teased Arab-Americans, calling them "dirty Iranians." The taunting youngsters were not to blame. They received their information about Arabs primarily from motion pictures, school texts, the comics, games and the television set.

The results of such stereotyping can be alarming. Dr. James Zogby, executive director of the American-Arab Anti-Discrimination Committee in Washington, writes: "Each year at our children's school there is a Halloween parade. The kids wear a variety of imaginative costumes and receive prizes. This year (1980), eight were dressed as ugly Arabs, wearing exaggerated noses, carrying oil cans and/or bags of money. On seeing this, my children were deeply upset. A short time later, at their school's ethnic festival, they argued against wearing their ethnic costumes."

The native Arab costume once conveyed a sense of pride. As a child, I remember wanting to wear a robe, headdress and sandals. It made me feel good to look like an Arab. Now Arab-American children may view Arab dress as a source of humiliation.

The first time I realized television's negative impact on children was on a Saturday afternoon in July 1976, when my daughter Michele and son Michael were watching that standard audience pleaser, *TV Wrestling*. "Daddy, Daddy," they called suddenly, "they've got some bad Arabs on." I rushed to the set in time to hear the ringside announcer say, "Akbar likes to hear the cracking of bones, and when he makes those faces, he is ugly, ugly!" "Akbar," said the announcer, "is from Saudi Arabia." The mere presence of the ruthless "Arab" in the ring heightened the frenzy of the jeering audience. But, in truth, this so-called scourge of the Middle East hailed from Texas.

Another "Arab" terror wrestling that afternoon was Abdullah the Butcher, a dirty fighter who openly enjoys inflicting pain on his opponents. Abdullah, billed as an Arab from the Sudan, is actually a black-American.

Michele and Michael were only six and seven years old when Akbar and Abdullah pinned their wrestling foes with "camel locks" in St. Louis. It was for them an unpleasant awakening. Their observations of the Arab TV image over the years has helped make this chapter possible. Their cry of "Daddy, Daddy" whenever the TV set glowed became a summons to watch "bad Arabs."

As we documented these caricatures, I explained to them that the Arabs they had met were the true Arabs. I mentioned some notable Americans with Arab roots: consumer advocate Ralph Nader; UPI White House reporter Helen Thomas; entertainer Danny Thomas; disc jockey Casey Kasem; and singer-composer Paul Anka. I also told them about some Arab-American sports figures: Salameh Hassan, Muhammad Ali's trainer; Joseph Robbie, principal owner of the Miami Dolphins; and former pro football star and coach of the Chicago Bears, Abe Gibron. TV Arabs are not real, I said, just stereotypes. Even today, when my children try to explain to their classmates that Arabs are just like other people, some students tease them. Arab is not "in."

Children often see their heroes defeat lame-brained Arabs on magic carpets in cartoons with an Arabian Nights setting. Their knightly actions subdue monstrous genies, crush corrupt rulers, and liberate enslaved maidens. Some animated shows revealing perceptions of sameness are *Richie Rich, Mork and Mindy, Scooby-Doo, Laurel and Hardy, Laverne and Shirley, Fonz and the Happy Days Gang, Bugs Bunny, Porky Pig, Popeye, Plastic Man, Heckle and Jeckle, Woody Woodpecker* and *The Superfriends.*

Wonder Woman rescues the Superfriends from "the inner world of a genie's lamp."

Woody Woodpecker stuffs a ruthless genie back into his bottle.

Popeye's muscles humble Arab fighters.

Heckle and Jeckle pull the rug from under "the desert rat."

Plastic Man flattens an Arab sultan with "egg in the face."

Porky Pig, in *Ali Baba Bound*, dumps a blackhearted Arab into a barrel of syrup.

Bugs Bunny, in *Ali Baba Bunny*, escapes from being "boiled in oil" by satisfying the whims of a sheik's story-hungry nephew—"the son of an unnamed goat."

Fonz saves Princess Charisma from the clutches of her Uncle Abdul—"Abdul-O, the Un-Cool-O," says Fonz.

Laverne and Shirley stop oil-sheik Ha-Mean-Ie from conquering "the U.S. and the world."

Laurel and Hardy rescue a heroine held hostage in Aba Ben Daba's harem.

Mork and Mindy are held hostage by Egyptians in a "pyramid snake chamber."

Richie Rich topples an outlandish sheik.

Scooby and his pals outwit Uncle Abdullah and his slippery genie.

In another *Scooby-Doo* show an Arab magician, on seeing Scooby, boasts: "Just what I've been waiting for. Someone to work my black magic on." He wants to turn Scooby into a monkey. But his magic backfires. The Arab, himself, becomes a monkey. Chuckles Scooby: "That mixed-up magician was sure sorry he monkeyed around with us."

What if Americans, not Arabs, were being trounced? How would we react if Arab nations portrayed cartoon characters—woodpeckers, dogs, rabbits and pigs—mugging Americans?

The anthropomorphic antics of these characters and others also reveal that corrupt sheiks and herds of veiled women are ubiquitous in Arabia.

In the past, harem life was *never* the prevailing custom in most Arab countries, notes the well-known Middle East scholar Dr. Philip Hitti. Today, harems are non-existent.

"The veil," notes Hitti, "may have had its origins in the context of protection rather than subjugation of women, its purpose being to shield her from the prying eyes of overzealous onlookers." The scholar estimates that "no more than ten percent of Arab women were ever veiled. "In many parts of the (Arab) world," says Hitti, "the veil has been unknown."

Fewer than five percent of the Arab people are Bedouins (desert dwellers), yet we often see them portrayed in children's shows as unfriendly nomads. By contrast, *The Empty Quarter*, a BBC documentary, reveals the traditional Bedouin hospitality, courage, honesty and endurance. *Empty Quarter* is based on the book, *Arabian Sands*, about Wilfred Thesiger's journeys in Arabia's harshest deserts between 1945 and 1950. Thesiger writes: "I have never met a Bedu (Bedouin) who was greedy, despite the hardship of their lives. A few years' relief from the anxiety of want was the most they ever hoped for." Continues Thesiger: "Other people will go to Arabia, but they'll move about in cars and they'll keep in touch with the wireless. They will, I believe, never know the spirit of the land or the greatness of the Arab."

Bedouin hospitality prevails today. While visiting one of Jordan's desert castles, an elderly, good-natured man approached my family and me. Aware that the desert heat had affected us, he was quick to show sympathy and welcomed us into his home—not a tent, but a small, modern concrete dwelling. We sat comfortably on ornate embroidered pillows. His warm smile reached out—stranger to stranger—as he prepared sweet tea on a gas burner. After several gulps we felt refreshed and stayed to chat for a while, neither knowing the other's language well. He seemed to enjoy our modest attempts to speak his language. After I thanked him for his hospitality, the Bedouin took out a single-string instrument and sang in a quivering voice filled with emotion. At that moment, I felt, as he did, that all men are brothers. This Arab from Jordan's desert touched our hearts. As we departed, he said, "Allah ma'ek," literally "God go with you."

In addition to relying on Bedouins as heavies, children's cartoon shows also gush forth with a line-up of evil genies, prowling mummies, conniving Arabs and mythical Arab kingdoms. One scheming Arab, Sheik Farout, appears in a *Tennessee Tuxedo* episode. Farout tries to destroy thousands of French Legionnaires with a watch that's actually a time-bomb. Thinking the watch is a gift, a Legionnaire readily accepts it as a token of Farout's friendship. But the lead character's dog outwits Farout by throwing the watch into the Arab's tent, where it explodes.

In the *Speed Racer* program "Race Against Time," a host of evil-eyed Egyptians led by Spint Femer endanger the lives of two heroic characters, Speed and Trixie. Femer's men try to burn Trixie alive, and launch a mammoth mechanically-operated Sphinx to crush Speed. Undaunted by such villainy, Speed saves Trixie, smashes the Sphinx, and easily defeats Femer's men.

Again, Egypt is the setting in a *Scooby-Doo* episode, where a mummy chases Scooby and his buddies. This same mummy, they suspect, turned their friend, the Egyptian archeology professor, Dr. Naseeb, into stone. Eventually, Scooby outmaneuvers the mummy's grunting clutches and dumps him into a basketball net.

When Scooby unveils the mummy, we see that it is not an ancient relic of Egypt's past, but simply a current example of Egypt's present. It's Dr. Naseeb, who is not stone after all. Naseeb posed as a mummy because he wanted to steal a valuable coin Scooby had found. Naseeb's greed, however, was his undoing—thanks to Scooby.

Another two-faced greedy Arab appears in the *Jonny Quest* program "The Curse of the Anubis." This urbanized Egyptian dignitary, Dr. Ahmed Kareem, steals the ancient statue of Anubis, claiming: "The God of Anubis belongs to all the Arab people."

Pretending to be friends with Dr. Quest, Jonny's father, Kareem invites him to visit some Egyptian ruins. When Dr. Quest questions the Egyptian's right to explore in the area, Kareem says: "In the Middle

East, borders are fluid affairs." The implication is that so are friendships. Kareem proceeds to lock Quest in a sealed crypt and lets loose three poisonous adders. Dr. Quest sighs, "This is a cruel country, at least by our standards."

Meanwhile Jonny and his dog, Bandit, easily outwit some nasty-looking Arabs in a jeep and scare off Arab guards at the ruins. The cowardly guards run frantically from a "god" that is actually Bandit.

The Egyptian is about to kill the Quests when a roving mummy appears; it throws Kareem against a wall, causing a cave-in which kills him. Says Dr. Quest, "Kareem found out there was a curse (on the statue) after all." Such is the fate of deceiving Egyptian explorers who fool around with Western adventurers like the Quests.

Unlike cartoon Arabs, real-life Arabs enjoy exploring and preserving geological and archeological wonders. One noted explorer, Dr. Farouk El-Baz, is Director, Center for Earth and Planetary Study, National Air and Space Museum, Smithsonian Institution. He is the geologist who once supervised lunar explorations for Bell Laboratories. El-Baz was one of those who chose the landing sites for the Apollo lunar-mission astronauts. It was he who taught the moon explorers what geological specimens to look for and photograph. And it was El-Baz the astronauts were addressing when they radioed from outer space such messages as, "Tell the King we're bringing him something from that little crater." (What else but "the King" would American colleagues call an Egyptian whose first name is Farouk?)

In a *Tales of the Gold Monkey* episode producers show a potpourri of stereotypes. The scene: A Japanese island. Inhabitants: Superstitious Egyptians that worship dogs. Super Villain: An American—of sorts. He's "half-Egyptian." Plot: Super Villain stirs up Egyptian islanders against show's heroes. Solution: Hero's dog, Jack, becomes the islander's new idol. Scores of Egyptians remain prostrate in Jack's presence. Dog and heroes escape.

"The Mystery of King Tut's Tomb," a *Hardy Boys* teleplay, suggests that viewers would be wise to stay away from Egypt. In it, Arabs kidnap young American girls and try to palm off fake artifacts. As in *Jonny Quest, Scooby-Doo* and other cartoons, the Hardy Boys, Joe and Frank, encounter scheming heavies with the single exception of an honest and intelligent Egyptian police officer. The boys become wary of Egypt when they hear that Egyptians imprison American students for eight years without a trial if they are caught with contraband and that pickpockets roam the streets of Cairo. At one point, the heavy in the show, Moustapha, warns a kidnapped American girl that unless she cooperates, he will make her "scream in pain." But Joe and Frank outfight and outwit Moustapha and his henchmen. They depart with the police officer's help. The officer is a welcome addition to this farfetched drama, albeit a "second banana" to the Hardy Boys. One doubts the boys will ever return to TV's Egypt.

Egypt is not a nation populated with pickpockets and swindlers. In fact, the country is comprised of people who take pride in their culture and in their long and honorable history. Egypt established itself as a cradle of civilization some 6,000 years ago. It is the oldest national state in the world, and the most heavily populated of all Arab countries. Throughout the past two centuries, Egypt has endured European military invasion, occupation and exploitation of its natural resources. Since the 1952 revolution through which it regained independence, Egypt has been struggling to modernize its economy and to improve the living standards of its enormous population. New industries, agricultural projects, social services and 12 state universities are well underway. In contrast to the *Hardy Boys* program, Westerners do not serve eight years in jail without a trial; women do not fear abduction from Cairo's crowded streets.

Cairo, the Egyptian capital with a population of over nine million, is a cosmopolitan Arab city where one experiences poverty and prosperity, past and present. The view from atop the Mosque of Mehemet, or any one of Cairo's multi-storied international hotels, presents a panorama of contrasts: pyramids, construction cranes, minarets, neon billboards, palm trees, modern office buildings, traditional sail boats and modern steel ships.

The city's traditional animated *souqs* (markets) offer unforgettable sights, sounds and tastes. There you can buy sweet tea and ice cold Pepsi, elaborate hand-crafted pieces of silver and gold and imported trinkets from Hong Kong. Along the winding stone streets, you can hear the tap-tap of the hammering craftsmen repairing shoes and making furniture and toys.

"Ahlan wa Sahlan" ("Welcome, this is your home.") is spoken as often as "good morning" in Cairo or in villages outside the city. The Egyptian people are deeply religious. Each day at sunrise, noon, mid-afternoon, sunset and nightfall, when the muezzin's voice chants the call to prayer—"Allah O Akbar!" ("God is Great!")—from the mosque, men and women in fields, in their homes, wherever they are, fall to their knees, bow their heads toward Mecca, and utter prayers of thanksgiving. Some of Egypt's people never converted to Islam. Yet, they live peacefully with their Moslem neighbors.

On television, however, Arabs are seldom portrayed as devout individuals, or even kind ones. Remember the mid-60s *Tarzan* series with Ron Ely? As TV's Tarzan, Ely was noble and strong, and constantly saving people from savages, wild animals—and Arabs.

I saw many *Tarzan* episodes with my children, some of which portrayed Arabs as slave masters. In one *Tarzan* program, "Bazzle of the Buldge," Arabs capture young blacks, sell them as slaves, and murder black men and women who resist slavery. The Arab leader tells Tarzan that his father and his father's father have always supplied slaves. "We have had a good life," he boasts. Tarzan halts the heartless slave trade and frees the young blacks, but not before he disables the Arab ringleader's getaway truck. "If I know these people, there's not a mechanic in the lot," Tarzan says.

I had to laugh back at that one. It reminded me of the time some friends were driving to Amman, Jordan, on some rough desert roads. Suddenly the car's warning light flashed. They lifted the hood and saw an empty radiator with a tiny hole. An hour passed, then a Jordanian truck driver came to their rescue. He gave them some drinking water and studied the damaged radiator. Then he took out his repair kit—egg with cement.

To their astonishment, the trucker mixed egg white with dry cement and formed a small moist ball. Then he neatly squished the ball into the small hole. Noticing the worried look on my friends' faces, he showed them patches of cement-egg fillings that dotted his own truck's radiator.

Unfortunately, my friends moved on before the cement was dry and the warning light reappeared. They encountered another trucker who checked the radiator, smiled and took out a jar containing large chunks of pepper. The trucker poured the pepper with a little water into the radiator to help seal the hole. "Start the car and let it run," he said. "You have no more problems."

My friends arrived safely in Amman. The next day they took the car to an auto shop, thinking the radiator would need additional work. Such was not the case. Instead, the mechanic looked under the hood and exclaimed, "I see you discovered truckers."

But rarely if ever are Arabs portrayed in TV shows like Jordan's clever and helpful truckers. Even some of the most distinguished children's authors have used Arab lands as settings for intrigue and villainy and made Arab rulers out to be hopeless, hapless heavies. Such was the case with the 1980 cartoon special *Pontoffel Pock, Where Are You?*, by the outstanding children's author Dr. Seuss. The author, whose real name is Dr. Theodor Seuss Geisel, is best known for his works *The Cat In The Hat* and *The Grinch Who Stole Christmas*. *Pontoffel* is a musical cartoon about a youth named Pock, a likeable bungler who wants to "get away from it all." Some magical fairies with Irish brogues grant Pock his wish, offering him a flying piano which can take him to mythical kingdoms.

Pock goes first to a place called Groogen, Seuss's version of a peaceful Tyrolian community where the townsfolk sing, play music and enjoy beautiful surroundings. Next he visits the fantasy Arab kingdom of Cashmopolis. Middle Eastern music underscores Pock's arrival. We see people sleeping, a juggler and then Neefa Feefa, who is billed as the greatest eyeball dancer in the world. For Pock, it's love at first sight. But Neefa must leave him to perform at the Arab ruler's palace. A citizen warns Pock not to go there, "It's out of bounds."

Undaunted, Pock goes to the palace and sees Neefa dance for the fat ruler, who sits atop huge pillows and smokes a water pipe. The veiled Neefa sings a song of remorse, "How I hate working for this royal slob." Pock and his piano fly to her rescue. The ruler shouts, "Guards!" We see that he is toothless as well as ugly. Pock escapes, but the king locks Neefa in a tower in the middle of the desert. Eventually, Pock's heroics free her from the king's clutches, and all, except maybe the ruler, live happily ever after.

Seuss himself is a great humanist. This we know through his writings. He did not have to ridicule Arabs or any other ethnic group to produce an entertaining cartoon show. *Pontoffel Pock* could easily have featured benevolent Arabs. If the author needed some bad guys, he could have offered some of his wonderful fantasy creatures.

Consider an alternate scenario for what *Pontoffel Pock* could have been: The King is handsome and intelligent, not backwards. His palace is open, never closed, to his people. The king loves Neefa and she him. But, alas, he suffers from shyness. Enter Pock. As matchmaker, he plays romantic ballads on his magic piano and presto—Neefa's and the king's hearts merge. This scenario offers children not villainy but love. The story could conclude with a gala wedding celebration.

Sometimes television writers who adapt original works for television have written in derogatory references to Arabs where none had existed before. This is what happened with the otherwise notable 1979 television special *The Kid From Left Field*, the story of a young bat boy (played by *Diff'rent Strokes'* Gary Coleman) who helps the San Diego Padres win the World Series. The team's manager, played by Ed McMahon, intent on selling the team and finding a buyer, says at one point, "I wonder if the Arabs like baseball." The original version of *Left Field* released in 1953 does not mention Arabs.

In Los Angeles, I met with NBC's Vice President of Broadcast Standards, Jerome Stanley, and discussed McMahon's statement.

"What was wrong with it?" Stanley wanted to know.

"Well, it was like, we'll give it to the Arabs. They're the ones with all the money," I replied.

Stanley replied, "Where else would you go if you were looking for somebody that might want to buy a baseball team, that has a lot of money, a lot of cash? Where is all the money at this point? Not all the money, but where is there a lot of money?"

The line in *Left Field* is more than an exaggeration of Arab wealth. Baseball is not even a typical sport in the Middle East. Baseball team owners would probably hesitate to approach Arabs with a sale offer. Would sports fans in a major American city cheer for a team that had been bought with Arab money?

One need just look at the example of the sports teams at Imperial Valley College in Imperial, California. Since the college was founded in 1922 the teams have been nicknamed "The Arabs." The college is now considering changing the name. Coach Mike Swearington told *Sports Illustrated* that when the football team traveled to Las Vegas, their bus carried the sign saying, "The Arabs Are Coming." "As I stepped off, I heard a guy say, 'What in the hell are Arabs doing here?' " Swearington said. When he tried to explain that "Arabs" was the team's nickname, the man snickered, "If that's your idea of a joke, it's in poor taste."

The coach said he believes the newly troublesome nickname has to go. The school's newspaper has already changed its name from "The Arab Mirror" to "The Mirror."

As my children grew into their teens, their TV viewing shifted to more advanced family programs, adventure and comedy, like the *Six Million Dollar Man, Bionic Woman, Tenspeed and Brownshoe* and *Fantasy Island.*

In the *Fantasy Island* show called "The Sheik," a meek school teacher befriends some Arabs and becomes a macho man. His dream fantasy, complete with harem, comes true—so he believes. Harem-maidens giggle, scratch his back, massage his feet and perform fiery dances. Unknown to the aroused teacher, besides belly dancing, there's a booby trap.

A friend tells him, "The old sheik set you up for assassins." When the bullies arrive, daggers and scimitars flash. Hakim, the harem-keeper, cracks his whip. The teacher fends off the double-crossing

Hakim and other attackers by using the sheik's bedpan as a shield. Scimitars are no match for a bedpan. The blades fall to the floor and the teacher easily escapes.

In one *Tenspeed* episode entitled, "It's Easier to Pass an Elephant Through the Eye of a Needle than a Bad Check in Bel Air," actor Ben Vereen sets the scene for his own "Arab scam." At a posh Bel Air hotel, Vereen passes himself off as a wealthy sheik. But on entering the sheik's suite several bodyguards corner him. The men wear TV Arab robes, carry sabers and can't speak English. Skulking in the background, they emerge to grunt and grin sheepishly for comic relief.

Although Vereen can't outfight the Arabs, he certainly can outwit them. He uses elementary tricks that most children would perceive as childish. Vereen plays with the dimmer switch, clicks the radio on and off and sings "Hickory Dickory Dock," "Hi Diddle Diddle" and "Jack Be Nimble."

Astonished by such hocus-pocus feats, the bodyguards say "Ahh Allah," and ooh and ahh. Vereen's partner witnesses this charade and asks, "How can they be so civilized and yet so primitive?" Replies Vereen, "They're from the desert. This is the first time they've seen a light bulb."

The bionic champions of freedom, Steve Austin and Jaime Sommers, frequently face foolish Arabs bent on creating world chaos. In "Return of Deathprobe," Steve must deliver two nuclear bombs to a Middle Eastern diplomat named Mahmoud or suffer the wrath of Deathprobe, an invincible machine capable of destroying thousands of innocent people in Colorado. Mahmoud intends to use the nuclear device to overthrow his cousin, King Faud. This tired Arab-versus-Arab theme focuses on Steve trying to stop the Middle East from "going up in smoke." Thanks to Steve, Mahmoud is captured and Deathprobe does not trigger a holocaust.

Jaime Sommers also copes with Arabs seeking to misuse nuclear weapons. In *Bionic Woman*'s two-part episode, "Father of the Cobalt Bomb," government leaders warn all nations not to explode thermonuclear bombs in the atmosphere. If such a test takes place, a nuclear physicist promises to detonate a doomsday device that will destroy the world. All nations but one comply with the governments' order not to explode an H-bomb: an Arab country disregards the warning and tests a hydrogen bomb. Apparently the explosion will cause the feared holocaust. But the physicist was bluffing—there was no doomsday weapon. This nuclear theme reinforces the notion of the Arabs' social irresponsibility and human insensitivity. Unknown to many viewers, no Arab nation currently possesses nuclear weapons. Only one Middle East country possesses nuclear capacity—Israel.

In another program about Arabs, "Jaime and the King," Jaime teaches Sheik Ali Ben Gazim how-not-to-be-a-male-chauvinist. This bionic program also perpetuates a falsity that Arab women are docile mistresses. One of Sheik Ali's aides asks, "Have you made a choice for tonight?" Glancing at his four mute and scantily-clad wives, the sheik sighs, "None of them. They all fail to amuse me."

Jaime asks to speak with Sheik Ali—"alone." Says Ali with four women by his side, "We are alone. This is my wife. And this is my wife." He explains to Jaime that he is allowed four, "officially, not including dancing girls and concubines." Ali prefers Jaime over his wives. But when she rejects his overtures he says "[Arab] women know their place. We men know what is good for them."

Jaime advises, "Your women could be unique if given the opportunity." Wives should not bow when they approach their husbands, she says. Reluctantly, the sheik promises "to put an end to that routine." His women "will stand erect, like men."

At his home in north Los Angeles, executive producer of the bionic series, Harve Bennett, told me why Arab women appear as belly dancers. "In television one tends to reach for beach-party-bingo-sex," he said. "When one has the opportunity to show a sexual image without being sexual, you usually seize upon it. You can see the belly dancer in the promo spots." The stereotype, Bennett added, "is a cliche; it saves the writer the ultimate discomfort of having to think. The greatest evil in television is that you are not asked to do in-depth material. You're asked to do something that can be quickly condensed and therefore cliches are often relied upon. Cliches, like headlines, are instantly identifiable."

But cliches may also be identified with positive images. Why not have Steve or Jaime befriend Arabs? Since Steve is a pilot, he could meet an Arab flying ace who teaches him something about precision flying. The writer could focus on the dangers involved. Such a program could be both entertaining and dramatic. As for Jaime, perhaps she could be introduced to an Arab woman who shares humanistic values. Together the two women could capture international culprits and reform corrupt leaders.

At least one *Six Million Dollar Man* episode, however, does somewhat depart from the typical Arab-as-heavy image. An Arab character, Sakari, and an Israeli character, Levy, are involved. Sakari, the target of an assassination plot, is overbearing and backward thinking. He tells a woman test pilot who tries to offer him advice, "Be quiet, woman," and reminds her that in his country "women have to walk behind the men." Levy also is an unlikeable person, who drinks too much and is quick to make snide remarks. In the end, Levy helps save Sakari's life; both men, Arab and Jew, embrace in the final scene. Antagonism turns to mutual respect. This refreshing plot avoids the standard good Israeli/bad Arab formula. Instead, we see two men with character flaws, who overcome past prejudices to develop a better understanding of each other.

The Arab-versus-Jew theme reappears, unfortunately, in the NBC annual Christmas special, *The Little Drummer Boy*, a household favorite for the past several years. Written by Romeo Muller, narrated by Greer Garson, and backed by the Vienna Boys Choir, *Drummer Boy* is also shown in elementary schools throughout the country. Writer Muller could have made *Drummer Boy* a tool to foster understanding. Instead, he opts for hackneyed characterizations. Muller's story is about Aaron, a frail youth who wears a yarmulke and fears people because his parents were killed by shepherd bandits. It is also the story of two shysters, Ben and Ali. Ali dons a fez while Ben wears a headdress. Ben has a protruding nose and oversized lips and carries a scimitar in his belt. He has "gold and silver on his mind, mischief in his soul," the script says. On meeting the poorly-clad Aaron, Ben, who will deceive anyone for wealth, exclaims, "We can be rich if he will play his drum for the crowd in the market place."

At the market square, Ben introduces some Arab performers. They are flops. Onlookers jeer as one of the jugglers fails to catch a jug and it breaks on his head. The restless crowd is about to disperse when Aaron's drum music wins back their attention. What a difference between Aaron and the hapless juggler!

In another scene, Ben encounters the Wise Men on their way to Bethlehem and forces Aaron to sell them his camel. The Wise Men pay Ben handsomely. His quest for gold now fulfilled, he and Ali no longer have need for Aaron.

In Bethlehem, a carriage runs over Aaron's lamb, Baba. Crying, Aaron cuddles Baba and takes him to the infant Jesus' manger. There, he offers the Christ child a gift of love—a song on the drum. Baba recovers and love replaces Aaron's hatred. The special concludes with the camera focusing on the shining star of Bethlehem as narrator Greer Garson says, "Blessed are the pure in heart, for they shall see God."

Drummer Boy permits viewers to have empathy for Aaron but not for Ben and Ali. Muller does not permit them, like Aaron, to change for the better on Christmas Eve. What a refreshing program *Drummer Boy* might have been if Ben, Ali and Aaron could have been friends. The Arab men could have discovered what Aaron learned at Christ's manger—the meaning of the gift of universal love.

This Christmas special reminded me of a magazine cartoon of the late sixties that showed a frustrated teacher and her pupils preparing a Christmas skit. The girls were dressed as angels, the boys as shepherds. One boy with a pained expression anxiously asked his teacher, "I'm not an Arab, am I?" Like the *Drummer Boy* of the seventies, this cartoon of the sixties suggests that Arabs aren't angels, but scalawags.

I'm afraid this idea also shows up in an otherwise excellent production of the Children's Television Workshop, *The Electric Company*. This series helps youngsters strengthen their reading skills, with some dramatic good *vs* evil contrivances to sustain their interest. Letterman is a vigorous *Electric Company* hero who constantly rights the wrongs of Spellbinder, a short, grubby-looking villain who resembles those turbanned Arabs in the escapist Arabian Nights' films of the fifties and sixties. Arabic music precedes Spellbinder's appearances and underscores his unscrupulous deeds. The rogue constantly waves his magic wand and alters the spelling of words, generally causing mischief and generating confusion. One example: we see a man happily munching grapes and above him the word "grapes" is superimposed; suddenly, Spellbinder appears, grumbling, "I hate to see someone happy." He changes "grapes" to "apes." Now two apes begin teasing the man. Bad Spellbinder. Naturally, Letterman arrives, beats up Spellbinder, changes "apes" to "capes." Why does Spellbinder, a negative force, have to have Arab features?

"The Letterman animated segments," explains Dr. Edward Palmer, vice president for research at Children's Television, "are used to make a very specific educational point about the impact that changing single letters can have on the meaning of words." Dr. Palmer was unable to meet with me in New York, but he wrote saying that in the many years that the series has been on the air, my inquiry was "the first to suggest that any of the characters in the Letterman segments might be taken as a stereotype of a particular ethnic group."

"I believe I understand the basis of your criticism," said Palmer, "but after screening a couple of segments that contain Spellbinder, I have come to a somewhat different interpretation." He failed to specify his interpretation of Spellbinder. Instead, Palmer questioned how Spellbinder, as I interpreted him, "could have survived this long the scrutiny of our own Children's Television's ethnically diverse staff and advisors."

Palmer explained that *Electric Company* is out of production and broadcasting only in repeats. "It is totally unfeasible to consider elimination, revision, or alternate production at this time," Palmer said. He added that a cost analysis revealed that in order to remove and replace the Letterman-Spellbinder segments, assuming there would be no additional new production, "would require an amount of $250,000—$500,000 to remove the segment and $200,000 to replace it. That kind of money, of course, is not available," he said. Children continue to see Spellbinder five days a week in reruns. Palmer told me "no review or renewal of its elements is planned within the foreseeable future."

Producers at Children's Television generally portray other minorities realistically and with respect—especially in the internationally acclaimed series *Sesame Street*. At present, 26 million pre-school children throughout the Arab-speaking world watch *Shari' Ishrin*, the Arab equivalent of *Sesame Street*. Advisors from Children's Television work in Kuwait with Kuwaiti technicians, actors, actresses, writers and a number of educational consultants. That is why I was so surprised to see stereotyping of Arabs in the Spellbinder segments when the staff at Children's Television has first-hand, on-site knowledge of contemporary Arabs.

Like Palmer, CBS's Donn O'Brien, vice president of broadcast standards, was faced once with an animated Arab mischief-maker—a rascal that almost appeared in a public service advertisement on tooth care during *Captain Kangaroo*, CBS's award-winning children's series. The J. Walter Thompson Agency produced this ad which featured an Arab in the evil role of "Tooth Decay." To his credit, O'Brien found the ad totally unacceptable. He rejected the spot before it was telecast. He later told me the cost of removing the ad was not considered.

As we have seen, many children's programs' heroes and heroines have a right, if not duty, to "reform" backward characters from other cultures. This theme does a disservice to all cultures and closes children to the possibility that they might be able to learn something from other peoples.

One series that takes exception to ethnic stereotyping is *Big Blue Marble*. The program, a production of the International Telephone and Telegraph Corporation (ITT), attempts to promote international understanding between different cultures. *Marble*'s theme song reflects the intent of each episode:

The Earth's a Big Blue Marble when you see it from out there.
The sun and moon declare our beauty's very rare.

Folks are folks and kids are kids, we share a common air.
We speak a different name, but work and play the same.
We sing pretty much alike, enjoy spring pretty much alike.
Peace and love we all understand and laughter we use
the very same brand.
Our differences, our problems, from out there there's not much trace.
Our friendships they can place,
While looking at the face
Of the Big Blue Marble in space.

Big Blue Marble focuses on how children in different parts of the world live. Commercial and public television stations can air *Marble* free of charge, provided they run no commercials with it. Each show contains a Pen Pal announcement inviting viewers to correspond with other children around the world. To date, *Marble*'s computerized Pen Pal service has matched more than two million young writers.

Executive producer Robert E. Wiemer says that the program has been filmed in some fifty countries, and tries to "capture the ambience, the special quality of the culture . . . . We focus on the homes, the work, the play of the children and young adults in many lands." The guidelines are: "Show the world as it is, with no editorial viewpoint expressed or implied, and do not depict violence in any form."

Several *Marble* programs focus on youths in the Middle East, including those who live in Bahrain, Egypt and Morocco.

In Morocco, *Marble*'s camera followed young Ali, who wanted to purchase an Arab instrument similar to a guitar, called a *lutar*. A quality-made *lutar* is expensive and Ali did not have the money, so he tried to earn some. His father gave him land to work and Ali grew and later sold his vegetables at a typical Moroccan marketplace.

In the end Ali purchases a fine *lutar*. We see him and young village girls play and perform a traditional dance. Music, laughter and a sense of togetherness prevail in these and the *souk* scenes—all of which implies that perhaps Morocco isn't so mysterious after all.

In the segment on Egypt, Egyptian youths learn the art of weaving at a school near the pyramids. Later they work with their families harvesting the crops. From the fields they rush to a swimming hole— inner tubes and all. The visuals in this program are impressive. We see the colorful tapestries at the school where the children created their own designs. After the lessons, the teacher takes her students for a stroll through the village. A young girl helps her mother bake bread, others make pottery. The camera intercuts between shots of bread in the open-air ovens and youngsters glazing pottery in the kilns. The emphasis, in keeping with *Marble*'s theme, is on a community of people in school, at play and at work.

In the Bahrain program, *Marble* traces Abdullah, the son of a sheik whose uncle is the country's ruler. The writers show Abdullah studying English in a classroom and trying to cope with math. His chauffeur drives him home from school in a Rolls-Royce. Then he works with his math tutor, plays soccer with friends and learns the proper way to drink coffee in the presence of his elders. Abdullah, like other kids, loves candy; his favorite is *halawa*, similar to a sesame-seed health-food snack.

At the shipyards, Abdullah observes ship builders constructing *dhows*—single-masted ships. Later he and some friends go for an evening cruise. On the *dhow*, the young sheik removes his traditional robe and underneath the robe is a multicolored Adidas shirt.

The Bahrain segment continually shows young Sheik Abdullah learning to live in harmony with the past while preparing himself for the future. When Abdullah goes camping, he drives a dune buggy, not a camel. There are neither harems nor assassins awaiting him in the desert or at home.

In New York, *Marble* producer Bob Saidenberg told me, "We try to portray kids in a positive light. We don't run into the problem of stereotypes with *Marble*. Kids are kids."

I asked Saidenberg how television could stop ethnic stereotyping. He replied that "the networks have to first recognize there is a problem, and second, they have to be willing to do something about it . . . they're not going to listen unless it's hammered over their heads."

For all its excellence and awards, *Marble* is only one series. It cannot compete with scores of other programs whose heroes are engaging in conflict rather than fostering mutual understanding between peoples.

The bulk of Arabs projected to young teens and children are on the wrong side of these conflicts. The Lebanese poet Kahlil Gibran has written, "Children are the lamps that cannot be snuffed by the wind and the salt which remains unspoiled through the ages. They are the ones who are steadily moving toward perfection." But can youngsters "remain unspoiled" if they continue to watch TV programs that consistently help shape prejudices?

Is it easier for a camel to go through the eye of a needle than for an Arab to appear as a *genuine* human being?

Whatever happened to Aladdin's good genie?

Ask a child to define Arab. The response will best summarize the problems discussed in this chapter. To a child the world is simple, not complex. Good versus evil. Superman versus Arabs.

My children may never cheer for an Arab hero unless Arab villains are nearby. But their children may. In time the innocence of childhood will triumph over the ignorance of man.

Most television executives are not insensitive to the importance of realistic images. In my meetings with them, I was not seeking a romantic ideal in which only good Arabs appear before young viewers. Instead I sought merely a balance in which courageous figures could work side by side with a youngster's cartoon heroes and the Bionic superstars.

Private Eyes and Police

We move now to television's staples, private eyes and police shows, which, unlike the programs already discussed, attract at least as many adults as children.

Throughout the years, the ingredients of melodrama—the chase, the escape, the arrest, the trial, the threat, the heroic sacrifice, the arraignment of vice and the last-minute rescue—have remained the same, though technology has changed drama somewhat. The stage is now a television set. Swords and charging cavalry horses have given way to high-powered rifles, high-speed car chases and helicopters. What hasn't changed is the basic melodramatic insistence on *action!*

The image of the private detective is solidly anchored in the American psyche. It connotes an extraordinary individual with penetrating intelligence and sharp intuition. Most of these private detectives are more efficient at solving crimes than the local police. They may get roughed up now and then, but they always manage to recover in time to solve their case.

Working from a refurbished office or an expensive convertible, their intuition, rather than scientific aids, gives them the upper hand. Today's television private eyes—Matt Houston, Simon and Simon, Jim Rockford, Barnaby Jones, Jonathan and Jennifer Hart, Frank Cannon and Simon Templar (The Saint)—are the modern incarnations of the early Errol Flynn heroes. Quite frequently we find them in the shadow of mosques and pyramids or in mysterious sheikdoms confronting bestial types who would willingly kill family members for "the cause," honor or the throne.

One private detective who frequently outwits Arabs is Frank Cannon. The balding, portly, middle-aged detective played by William Conrad, relies on his wits rather than his muscle. In one episode he helps a young Arab student whom police have accused of being a drug smuggler and murderer. Besides Cannon, only an Arab math teacher and the youth's girlfriend believe in the student's innocence. Cannon eventually catches the killer—the math teacher.

In another *Cannon* segment, Prince Ahmed of the Kingdom of Kashir is kidnapped. His abductors demand a ransom of $5 million. When they don't get it, their leader says Ahmed will be murdered. Ahmed's brother, Prince Hassan, arrives in time to bump off the kidnappers. Then he goes to his brother with a gun, not an embrace. Hassan wants the throne for himself. But Cannon prevents the violence. "You kill your brother and we'll send you home to your father and what he'll do to you, I wouldn't even want to think about."

Another *Cannon* program, "Tomorrow Ends at Noon," depicts the love between a Palestinian man named Hassan and an Italian woman. Hassan takes his bride-to-be not to a chapel but to a tramp steamer. It seems Hassan is involved with a group of Palestinians who are seeking the release of some hijackers, and who hope to use the girl's abduction as leverage in getting the others freed. But Hassan's Palestinian "friends" imprison him too, fearing that he really loves the woman and will betray "the cause" for her. At one point, one of the Palestinians tells Hassan's guard, "Hassan is your cousin. It may be necessary to kill him." The guard replies, "As the cause demands, Colonel."

The woman's father has influence with the Italian government but refuses to cooperate with the Palestinians for the release of the hijackers in exchange for his daughter. The Palestinian colonel warns him that unless Italian authorities meet his demands, "We will cut your daughter's throat." Cannon, who just happens to be in Italy, commends the father for his courageous position. "Those four terrorists in jail killed half a dozen people in a Naples airport," he says. Thanks to Cannon's heroics, the woman is eventually rescued, the Palestinian colonel killed and Hassan jailed.

These Cannon episodes point up three major misconceptions: 1) Arabs are not trustworthy (for example, the Italian father warns his daughter to stay away from Hassan); 2) Arabs would kill even blood relatives (a cousin is ready to kill another cousin "as the cause demands"); 3) all Arabs are the same. "They all look alike..." cautions Cannon's companion after a group of Arab cooks try to chop Cannon up with a butcher knife. This comment reflects an unpleasant yet all too familiar diatribe.

Do Blacks, Jews, Orientals, Italians and others "all look alike?" One merely has to look at my cousins, Salem Green and Charlie George, for a clue. After serving, like many other Arab-Americans in World War

II. my cousins returned to Clairton, Pennsylvania, where they became policemen. Salem is tall, thin and has blue eyes. Charlie is short, boasts a protruding stomach and has brown eyes. They neither look nor think alike. On their neighborhood beats, these men were accepted and welcomed as part of the community. If Salem and Charlie suffered, it was not from ethnic slurs, but from the hospitality of housewives who insisted that they sample their freshly-baked breads and pastries. Salem and Charlie were Clairton's "good guys."

When I was interviewing television executives about the casting of Arabs, I again ran into this notion that TV Arab characters must all look dark, swarthy and somewhat sinister to be believable. *Cannon*'s producer, Anthony Spinner, told me about the problem he faced when he tried to cast some real Arab actors for roles in an episode of *The Saint*, another private eye series. Some of the Arabs had blue eyes and this upset Spinner's boss, Quinn Martin, who told him, "Arabs don't have blue eyes." Spinner said he explained to Martin that the actors were natives of Jordan and Egypt. But, Spinner said Martin replied, "I don't care. They may be real Arabs and Arabs may have blue eyes. But that's not what the American people think they look like."

Although the *Cannon* series passed into "video heaven" in the mid-70s, ABC resurrected William Conrad in a 1980 drama, *Turnover Smith*. Smith, a famed investigator, uses computer technology to track down criminals. In one episode, he tries to catch a crazed strangler whose victims include an American Army colonel's wife. Two Arab "terrorists" give the colonel $250,000 in cash for top-secret documents. (Who has more money than TV Arabs?) The terrorists see the strangler entering the complex where the colonel lives. Then the strangler murders the colonel's wife. When the colonel arrives and sees his wife dead, he assumes the Arabs are responsible. A struggle ensues and the two terrorists kill him.

Fuad, one of Smith's international students, appears as an intelligent Arab who helps the investigator capture the terrorists and the strangler. At first, the Arabs refuse to identify the strangler as the man who killed the colonel's wife. Warns a fellow Arab, "You will be sent back to your country and within 24 hours your head will have no body." He suggests they "cooperate with the police here."

Constant references to beheadings could make viewers think this act of punishment is common practice. "Nothing could be further from the truth," explains Tareq S. Nabel, an expert of Arab legal matters. Nabel says that with the exception of Saudi Arabia, beheadings have not occurred in Arab nations for hundreds of years. And even in Saudi

Arabia, "beheadings are practically non-existent. Like your gas chamber and electric chair, such executions take place only when shocking and violent crimes are committed," he said.

Arab justice is basically the same as European justice. There are court proceedings and an attorney represents the accused. The state provides attorneys for the indigent. In some Arab countries, like Bahrain and Saudi Arabia, justice is doled out with a personal touch that exists in no other parts of the world. In these countries, citizens can air their grievances face-to-face with their rulers at open-door audiences known as *majlis*. Once held in tents in the desert, the *majlis* now take place in Saudi Arabia's modern palaces. King Kahled of Saudi Arabia opens the gates of his palace weekly, and princes in the country's various provinces hold almost daily sessions.

Like *Turnover Smith*, a number of private eye shows concern terrorism. Almost without exception, the Palestinians are portrayed as the terrorists. As an example, in one episode of producer Anthony Spinner's *Return of the Saint*, called "One Black September," the Saint, who is urbane, handsome and blessed with a halo for a calling card, is up against Palestinian assassins in England. He and Israeli agent Leila Sabin are after Abdul Hakim, a member of the militant Black September organization. Abdul is also being pursued by three fellow Palestinians, who threaten and rough up his girlfriend, Yasmina, and her father.

The Israeli's capture of Abdul is illegal, but the Saint and the British in general approve of the manhunt. When Leila, the cool-headed Israeli agent, confronts Yasmina about Abdul's whereabouts, the Arab woman behaves like a whimpering child.

Leila, on the other hand, is never less than courageous or independent. At one point, the Saint takes her to his apartment and wants to make love. But the sensuous Leila refuses romance, explaining that she must avenge the deaths of her family members, who were killed in a terrorist attack at an airport.

Three Palestinians eventually capture Leila and threaten to kill her. "Forget about me," she staunchly tells the Saint. "You've got Hakim." The Saint turns Abdul over to the Israelis, who tie the Palestinian to a chair and start working him over. "Do you really have to do it this way?" asks the Saint. "Hakim is a key acquisition in our struggle with the PLO," one of the Israelis replies.

The program concludes with the Saint freeing Leila from the clutches of Black September. Abdul pleads, "If I [confess] to them [the Israelis], I'm dead." Leila consoles him, "Well, at least you'll get a fair trial, which is more than you ever gave our people." But the Saint decides to free Abdul in exchange for more information about Black September agents. "That man has killed God knows how many innocent people and you have just let him walk out of here with his life," protests Leila. "Have I?" says the Saint. Then we hear the sound of gunfire near Abdul's getaway plane. His Palestinian "brethren" have followed him to the airport, just as the Saint expected they would, and assassinated him.

An Israeli colonel tells Leila and the Saint, "You both carry with you the deepest gratitude of the Israeli people." He gives them two tickets to Bermuda. Leila is happy. She has avenged the murder of her family. She can now make love. As for Abdul and other Palestinians, the moral of the show is: "The only good TV Palestinian is a dead Palestinian."

The show suggests that Palestinians are "terrorists." "September" not only lacks substance, it also reflects a biased view of the Middle East conflict: Israel—right; Palestine—wrong. The episode falsely implies that the PLO and Black September are the same organization. They are not. Only a few thousand Palestinians belong to Black September.

Conversely, the PLO is the national representative of the Palestinian people. Almost universally, Palestinians in exile and under occupation recognize the PLO as their representatives. So do 105 independent governments around the world as well as the United Nations. The PLO is in practice a de facto government-in-exile. This government has built schools, established factories and welfare systems. One department, the Red Crescent Society, runs more than 10 hospitals and 100 clinics.

Many Jewish leaders and organizations are currently seeking dialogue with the Palestinians. Nahum Goldmann, former president of the World Zionist Organization and an organizer of the World Jewish Congress, has publicly advocated meetings between Israelis and Palestinians. "I see no peace unless Palestinians are granted the right to build their own country as they want to," Goldmann has said.

Rabbi Alexander Schindler, president of the Union of American Hebrew Congregations, is another Jewish-American who openly professes compassion for the Palestinian people and understands their need for a homeland. "I feel almost a kinship with the Palestinians," he once told a *Time* reporter. "The role they are playing in the Arab world is not unlike the role of the Jews in the world—rootless wanderers."

A majority of Americans concur with Rabbi Schlinder and Nahum Goldmann. A 1982 national poll revealed that 76% of those questioned agreed with the statement: "The Palestinians have a right to have a state of their own;" just as much as the Jews deserved their own homeland after WW II.

The "September" show also pits the positive image of an Israeli woman against the negative one of an Arab woman. The contemporary Arab woman is seldom depicted realistically in television programs. In the minds of many viewers, the Arab woman's world is restricted to three things: the veil, seclusion and polygamy—all of which are blamed on Islamic tradition.

In "The Status of Women in the Arab World," Professor Shwikar Elwan writes that "Islam has been a liberalizing force" and has actually helped advance the status of women. Islam, she says, recognized a woman "as an independent being and gave her what was then, and is still considered to be, a liberal bill of rights and responsibilities." Islam allows a woman to keep her family name after marriage and grants her the right to own property and dispose of it freely, without the intermediary of a husband or male guardian, Dr. Elwan says. Islamic women had these rights, she notes, at a time when no female in Europe was allowed to own property on her own.

As for the veil and seclusion, Dr. Elwan notes that neither Islam nor pre-Islamic Arabia is responsible for them. Arabs borrowed the customs of the veil, seclusion and the harem from Turkish and Persian societies. Only beginning in the 12th century did women—both Christian and Moslem—begin wearing veils. The veil was then the symbol of upper class women, not a sign of inferiority. "The Bedouin women in North Africa and the peasant women in Egypt have never worn the veil," Dr. Elwan notes.

Today Arab women attend the same colleges and universities as men. Their jobs "over there" are pretty much the same as our jobs "over here." Many Middle East nations give the education of women high priority, and most schools throughout the Arab world are free. The rate of women's enrollment at all levels of educational institutions is growing faster than that of men. In Jordan's main university, for example, female enrollment in the schools of Science, Islamic Law and Nursing exceeds fifty percent.

Women are becoming not only teachers and nurses, but scientists, architects, biochemists, doctors and pharmacists. In October, 1980, Jordan began a new pharmacy program with fifty-three students: forty-eight of them women.

In both Saudi Arabia and Qatar, where once no schools for girls existed, professional women find excellent work opportunities today. Fifty percent of Qatar's 34,000 students are female. More than half of its

2,500 teachers are women. In Saudi Arabia, the educational opportunities for both sexes are also impressive—of the country's six million inhabitants, more than 1.5 million are enrolled in school.

In most Arab countries women work *with* men. In Jordan, my friend Hayfa Abu Kurah served as project manager of the capital's new Jerusalem Hotel. For three years, Hayfa worked hand-in-hand with electrical engineers, carpenters and other construction workers. "They treated me as an equal," she said, "because I knew my job and they respected that."

The editor-in-chief of *The Middle East,* one of the most respected English language news magazines serving European and Arab lands, is a woman. Throughout the Arab world, I have met with women who are ministers of information, work as lawyers, professors, journalists, pharmacists, architects, hotel sales managers, dentists, doctors, co-pilots and flight engineers.

One example of interaction between the sexes takes place daily at Amman's Hai Nazzal Community Center. The young men and women who built the center are sociology students from Jordan University. Instead of seeking government grants and hiring contractors to do the job, the students and members of the community scraped the funds together themselves and decided to build the center on their own. The center, which serves under-privileged children and adults, is located in one of Amman's poorest sections, on land that had been a wheat field. Today the center includes an aviary, flower and vegetable gardens, a library and several classrooms. In one room, I saw women making handicrafts. In another, adults were learning to read and write. One housewife told me that Hai Nazzal had changed her life and outlook about herself. In this densely populated area where children have but dusty streets to play in, one little boy, dressed in a Boy Scout uniform, proudly spoke of how he loves books and the Scouts.

The young women I saw working at the center resembled fashion models. They wore stylish jeans, sweaters, boots, gold chains and bracelets. But they also hauled and unloaded cement, laid tile at the center's new outdoor amphitheater and dug gardens.

While women of all nations still encounter some discrimination, the advancement of Arab women has been remarkable. How realistic is it, then, to portray them as simple chattels?

I expressed my concern about such images in the various television series Americans see, or have seen, on prime time when I met with Tom Kersey and Don Bay at ABC's Office of Broadcast Standards and Practices.

"TV gives us flattering images of American women," I said. "Why can't we see some valorous Arab women?"

Bay mentioned *Vega$*, a series about a mod detective who attracts beautiful women and plenty of trouble as he dashes about in a flashy, vintage Thunderbird. He said that in one *Vega$* show, "The Visitor," an Arab woman is featured. "She's a young lady in a cocktail dress, just like everyone else," he said.

He pointed out that the woman and her statesman father are positive characters, "balanced by some negative characters from their country who are trying to overthrow their government."

Bay arranged for me to screen "The Visitor." The show opens with a newspaper headline reporting a potential civil war in Princess Lelya's country as she arrives in Las Vegas. Private eye Dan Tanna tries to protect Lelya from fanatics who seek to overthrow the Arab government headed by her father. An Arab heavy named Hammad is hired to kill her father. He advises his accomplices, "Whatever happens, remember your vows. None of you is to be taken alive."

Later one of the plotters fails in her attempt to assassinate Lelya. For this, Hammad shoots her. But before she dies she screams, "Long live the liberation." Dan and the police discover that the victim "was a fanatic from the Middle East who seemed to be a lady of mystery." Lelya, however, humanizes the girl's tragic death, saying, "In her own way she loved our country as much as I do."

Dan takes Lelya and his assistant Twoleaf to a nearby lake for a meal fit for a princess—hot dogs. Together they laugh over jokes and enjoy the countryside's peaceful solitude. Lelya explains that there may soon be civil war in her country because her father and his opponent, Jafai, are both proud, stubborn men. They were once very close, she says, but Jafai, a religious man, thinks the country is changing too rapidly. He accuses Lelya's father of trying to transport simple tribesmen into the space age.

The program treats the Islamic religion with reverence. Instead of cliches, the writer uses examples of what Arabs actually say to each other. For instance, when Lelya departs the hotel to meet with Jafai, her friend says, "God go with Your Highness." On meeting Lelya, Jafai softly utters, "God is great." They share past memories of mutual respect. He was once her teacher and though she still admires him, she advises, "You were wrong to hold back history." Lelya also admonishes her father for being "too progressive." This scene is beautifully written and acted. It depicts negotiation for the first time with respect and admiration between an Arab woman and man.

Lelya carries a treaty of peace—one with compromise from both sides. At this point, however, Hammad and his henchmen appear and kidnap Lelya and Jafai. "I promise you both, the way you die will be of greatest service to our people," grunts Hammad.

Dan and Twoleaf arrive to thwart the attempted assassination. Dan punches out Hammad. Twoleaf mounts a forklift and chases the Arabs, pinning them against a picket fence. The segment concludes with Lelya, Dan and Twoleaf proposing a toast "to peace and friendship."

In *Matt Houston* and *Scarecrow and Mrs. King* episodes, we see similar themes. Kidnappers abduct the son of an Arab king in *Matt Houston*. The youth may be killed because the king lacks sufficient money to pay the ransom. Unlike most detective programs, the kidnappers here are not Arabs. The writer does not employ the standard Arab-against-Arab ploy. Instead, he focuses on traditional beliefs—friendship, religious devotion and the love of a father for his son.

Only one character mars the taut teleplay—Fahad, the king's brother. Fahad "wears bedsheets on his head," has a TV harem and flaunts too much money. He wants to pay $10 million for a modest restaurant—"price does not matter," he sighs.

In *Scarecrow and Mrs. King*, Arab bodyguards are mute and bewildered. Their princess goes off to see a children's play with Mrs. King and the guards panic. They burst into a crowded auditorium. The audience screams. The performing kids freeze, then slowly raise their hands over their heads—they fear it's a stick-up.

The princess explains that "Arab mothers don't do anything, especially talk or give opinions." She also shares anxieties with Mrs. King, "Do you know what it's like to have men with machine guns outside your door when you're in bed with your husband?"

In spite of the Arab heavies in *Vega$*, the ludicrous Fahad in *Matt Houston* and the bumbling bodyguards in *Scarecrow and Mrs. King*, the teleplays are entertaining. Two of the programs, *Matt Houston* and *Vega$*, offer examples of religious devoutness that are true to life. In Beirut, Lebanon, I once came upon an open air *souq* that featured hundreds of shops, selling everything from gold to shish kebab. In the heart of the *souq* was a small, enclosed chapel called *Souq En-Nouri* (Market of Light). Daily, men and women and children—Moslem and Christian—would pause and enter this place to light candles and say prayers.

In Jordan, I also saw Moslems devoutly express their faith. At midday, it wasn't unusual to see a taxi driver keep his passengers waiting as he removed a prayer rug from his car's trunk and knelt at the curb to pray and give homage to his maker. At sunset, businessmen often steer their cars off the highway, get out and kneel and pray. To date, most television programs fail to portray followers of Islam in this devout practice.

If there is one type of Arab woman who intrigues television writers, it is the adulterous wife. This popular theme pops up in a *Rockford Files* episode, "The Three Day Affair with a Thirty Day Escrow." The show begins with some Arab roughnecks dragging Rockford out of bed. Jim resents their pushing him around so early in the morning and throws a few solid punches, knocking them flat. Then he turns on a water hose and escapes.

Jim soon learns that his friend Sean precipitated the Arab attack. Sean was having an affair with a married woman—Khedra. Jim warned him to cool it: "Picture yourself hanging upside down while some Arab is picking your teeth." Sean says that Khedra is "an old-style Moslem wife—no matter what he [her husband] does, you sit and wait for your man." Khedra's husband has slept with a lot of other women, Sean says, but Khedra appears as the downtrodden slave of both her family and her husband.

When Khedra's father learns of the affair with Sean, he conducts a mock trial. On the table where her father, brother and two other relatives preside, there lies a copy of the *Koran*. The *Koran's* presence at the trial suggests the Arabs are only following "Islamic law." The father is stunned: "You let yourself be bedded by one man while married to another? ... If this is true, and you were not sick in any way (meaning mentally unbalanced at the time of the act), we must deal with you." Khedra has brought shame to the family. A relative advises: "She must be dealt with at home where she was born, not here in this country." Rockford is aghast. "Families are supposed to stick together," he says.

The Arabs, however, ignore his pleas and whisk everyone off to their private plane. Khedra will be executed in the Middle East. But not if Jim can help it. He creates confusion by setting off an explosion so he and Khedra escape. Khedra's father cannot stand the turmoil. He has a heart attack and dies. No one seems to notice his final gasps and no one grieves.

The episode concludes with Sean and Khedra thanking Jim. Being a wealthy Middle East princess, she insists that he accept a reward. He reluctantly takes her check, saying, "I don't know what to say." Jim smiles, anticipating a large sum of money, then frowns on seeing that the check is only for $125.

The *Rockford* show presents an Arab family as heartless and hateful. It suggests that if a married Arab woman sleeps around, her family will jet over to America, lock her in a room and condemn her to death. I asked *Rockford*'s Executive Producer Meta Rosenberg why the program portrayed Khedra's family as wishing to kill the princess. "It's a custom," she said.

This theme, the wife as chattel, also appears in a *Casablanca* program. Here, an Arab family conducts a hearing, complete with a copy of the *Koran*. If the wife is found guilty of adultery, her head will be "cut off." Following TV's Moslem law, family members threaten to "kill the offending woman and 'fix' the offending man."

While visiting several Middle East countries, I spoke with many men and women in villages and cities about what happens to a woman if she commits adultery. The consensus was that divorce generally occurs. Then the families usually try to convince the "adulterers" to marry. There is shame for the woman's family. But few women in Islamic nations are killed for committing adultery, just as few women in Western nations get killed over adultery.

Television would have us believe that Arabs treat women of their own kind harshly, and that they are twice as satanic with pretty young American girls. In that vein, white slavery is a favorite theme. In an episode of *Vega$*, actor Cesar Romero plays a ruthless man who lures women to yacht parties, drugs them, then flies them off to—where else?—Arabia. Romero tells one showgirl who is bound and gagged, "You as a person mean nothing to me, but your body and your looks are worth $25,000 to anybody who likes blond hair and straight teeth." At one point, he informs an associate, "We'll take this girl and the others and leave for the Middle East in our chartered plane."

In a *McCloud* episode, Sam McCloud (Dennis Weaver) confronts Arabs who whisk off American beauty-contestant finalists to the Kingdom of Aramy. The Arab heavy, Ramal, likes his women to be "blond, beautiful, young and innocent." He tells one captive: "When I return, you will be willing, docile and loving." If she refuses, Ramal will toss her into the bordello where another American "works." At 25¢ per customer, "business is booming."

Eventually, McCloud frees Aramy's enslaved women by knocking out several saber-wielding TV Bedouin-types with six solid cowboy know-how punches. Then he meets Aramy's ruler, Sheik Kimpal. McCloud reveals that Ramal is a white-slaver. We can only surmise Ramal's forthcoming punishment. Earlier, the sheik ordered guards to behead his nephew—"on the day of my birth."

The white slavery theme reappears in *Police Woman*, starring

Angie Dickinson as Pepper Anderson, the police sergeant who baits criminals with intelligence and good looks. In "The Young and the Fair," Pepper attempts to stop girls from being abducted to the Kingdom of Ramat. "They're a little young," one policeman says of the girls. "For people with normal taste," his companion replies.

An Arab studies professor, Salim Daoud (Rosanno Brazzi) seems to be the prime suspect in the show. While investigating the case, Pepper falls in love with him. Salim speaks five languages, is handsome and charming, a gourmet cook and an art historian. "You're not an ordinary Arab," Pepper says. "My mother was French," Salim replies.

Salim works, however, on the side of justice. In the final scene, he prevents an innocent 15-year-old from being forced into the arms of a seamy Arab prince, who smugly awaits her in his private helicopter. The show concludes with Salim extending Pepper an invitation to visit his homeland. "That's a beautiful thought," she says.

I asked writer Irving Pearlberg why he portrayed Salim, a sympathetic character, as only half-Arab. "He wasn't half-French in the original script," Pearlberg said. "Someone," he added, "maybe the director or producer wrote that into the script. My guess," he said, "is that someone upstairs who was involved with the show figured this man (Rosanno Brazzi) doesn't look like an Arab, so let's give him half-European ancestry."

There is a glimmer of hope in Pearlberg's story. It shows that at least one Hollywood writer is willing to create a character who is both a hero and a true-blue Arab.

But in a *Cagney and Lacey* episode the stereotype dominates.

We see the policewomen dupe the arrogant oil-rich Hassan Bin Moqtadi. The Arab drives a new Rolls-Royce, with the license plate, OILBUX, and runs over an American Jew, Saul Klein. Moqtadi has diplomatic immunity. He won't pay Klein's hospital bills, and he can't be arrested.

An angry Cagney says: "You know what ticks me off, inspector? In this guy's country you steal a piece of fruit off a cart and they cut your hand off. He comes over here (New York City) and . . .nearly kills a man. And we can't even touch him."

Cagney and Lacey call the Arab a "clown," and a "spoiled brat" with "crooked teeth." On visiting Moqtadi's Embassy, Cagney says, "I feel like I'm in the middle of the Arabian Nights." The women are served Arabic coffee and Lacey complains: "Ohhhh, how do they drink this stuff?" Caustically, Cagney says, "It's a ritual of politeness." The women laugh. Lacey then dumps her coffee into the nearest flower pot.

Eventually, Cagney and Lacey outsmart Moqtadi. The Arab agrees to pay Klein's hospital bills. And he gives the officers a $500 donation to a "worthy charity—the United Jewish Appeal."

We may applaud Cagney and Lacey's heroics and Saul Klein's humanism. But what do we think of Moqtadi's behavior?

What if the writer had reversed the role of the show's protagonists, Klein and Moqtadi? Would it be acceptable to telecast a program that shows a rich Jew running down a poor Arab? Would we see the Jew pay the Arab's hospital bill? And donate $500 to a worthy Arab charity? And would Cagney and Lacey discard bagels as they did Arabic coffee?

Some TV writers tend to fall back on traditional cliches. Since the 1920 motion picture *Little Egypt,* moans and murmurs from roving mummies and the hootchy-kootchy dance have become synonymous with Egypt and the Egyptians. One *Hart to Hart* program focuses on Assad, a crazed Egyptian mummy-keeper. Assad believes Jennifer Hart (Stephanie Powers) is a lost Egyptian princess and wants to return her to a dead prince. He drugs Jennifer with a secret potion, lays her out in a sarcophagus and prepares to plunge a golden blade into her heart; he advises: "Do not be afraid my princess. You will soon be united with your prince for all time." Fortunately, Jennifer's reunion with the mummy prince is averted.

One question I consistently asked television writers and producers was, how likely is it to see chivalrous Arabs on television in the near future?

CHiPs producer Cy Chermack told me, "I think it would not be impossible, but it would be difficult." Added Chermack, "In my series Jon and Ponch are the heroes of every program and sometimes they run into guys that are heavies." In one *CHiPs* episode, "The Sheik," the heavy was a reckless Arab playboy who tries to bribe the officers with bundles of $100 bills. Like the backward TV sheik of the desert, this irresponsible hot-rodding sheik of the freeway must be "educated." Ponch teaches him laws must be obeyed and that friendship cannot be bought.

Chermack told me, "The program may be offensive in some ways we're not aware of. If so, we'll try to mend our ways." Like most producers and writers, Chermack does not know many Arabs, or Arab-Americans, personally or professionally.

Producer Anthony Spinner said Arab heroes would not appear "until the oil prices are lowered, until there is peace in the Middle East.... Until it stops becoming a hot spot for corruption or killing." He did, however, say he thought it might be possible now to feature a heroic Egyptian, in light of Anwar Sadat's stunning reputation in this country. "But two years ago,' it would not have been possible," he said.

Spinner had some ideas about how a writer might work a positive Arab-American character into a television show. "Find a prestigious writer who would go to a network executive and say, 'I want to do this story...Here is an Arab pathologist who works in a Chicago hospital. And because of him—if this ever happened—forty-eight lives were saved.' " Such a plot has numerous possibilities.

There are more than 10,000 American doctors of Arab heritage specializing in various fields of medicine. Heart specialist Michael DeBakey is internationally known for the studies he has made in cardiovascular surgery. He has also invented more than fifty surgical instruments, including the heart-lung bypass pump that made open-heart surgery possible.

There are also Dr. Charles Kilo of St. Louis, Missouri, the four Mansour brothers of Jeannette, Pennsylvania, and Dr. Daoud Hanania of Amman, Jordan. Dr. Kilo is co-founder of the Kilo Diabetes and Vascular Research Foundation. The Mansour Medical Group opened their doors to war-wounded Lebanese children. Dr. Hanania heads the Queen Alia Heart Institute, the showpiece of Amman's 700-bed King Hussein Medical Center.

Entertainer Danny Thomas founded St. Jude's Hospital where children are treated for leukemia and other diseases. There are numerous examples of other modern-day Arab and Arab-American "good" guys which television writers could draw upon as prototypes for their heroes.

Meta Rosenberg, producer of *The Rockford Files,* told me she thought Arabs have not been portrayed more positively because "they are strange to us.... They are different." And, she said, this engenders hostility. Writer Irving Pearlberg says it is because "there are Arab oil billionaires at our expense.... Even though there are American oil billionaires at American's expense, people here generally don't look at it that way." Pearlberg says, "The Arabs are, unfortunately, a target because of a handful of oil billionaires who have as much right to be billionaries as anyone else." Television today, he says, could show a humane Arab, though not in a starring role.

At one time, producers, writers and network officials prevented blacks from having starring roles. Then, in 1965, NBC and producer Sheldon Leonard introduced the *I Spy* series. With that show, actor-comedian Bill Cosby became the first black to appear in a starring role in a regular dramatic series. He played an American espionage agent who had graduated from Oxford, spoke several languages and traveled around the world righting wrongs.

During the cold war, *The Man From U.N.C.L.E.* series (1964-68) featured a Russian super agent, Illya Kuryakin. The Russian and his American co-star, Napoleon Solo, saved the world from international villains—including Arabs. If TV can spotlight friendly and daring Russians, why not intrepid Arabs?

I believe Arabs should win the same kind of acceptance other ethnics have won. There is no doubt in my mind that as producers and writers learn more about Arabs and their culture, they will discover that Arabs—just like all the ethnic heroes of television private-eye and cop shows—are people who possess courage, wit, intelligence and charm. It is only when the *real* image of Arabs becomes known that the *reel* image will change.

Comedy

Often some of the best humor on television centers on the political climate and personalities of the day. The comedy of the Seventies and Eighties might well be dubbed the era of the Arab joke.

A major 1980 news story which engendered a host of Arab jokes was the FBI's ABSCAM (Arab Scam) caper in which FBI agents posed as Arab oil barons in an attempt to ensnare less than trustworthy politicians on Capitol Hill. A *New Republic* editorial noted that, "It's an unattractive reflection on society that a resort to crude stereotypes should be so acceptable and so effective at the upper reaches of government." *The New York Times'* editor A.M. Rosenthal remarked that he wouldn't have liked it if ABSCAM was dubbed JEWSCAM. In the ABSCAM caper FBI Director William Webster had two of his agents dress up in traditional sheik's garb. The agents had phony Arab names: Sheik Kambir Rachman from Oman and Sheik Yasser Habib from Lebanon. Why didn't politicans know they were being finagled? "Kambir" is not an Arab name; Lebanon has no oil sheiks.

The FBI investigation prompted countless ABSCAM jokes from the Senate cloakroom to *The Tonight Show* with Johnny Carson. *The Washington Post* reported that a Democratic senator sardonically asked his aide one day, "Any mail from Abdul Enterprises?" And Johnny Carson chuckled: "They say the bribes were filmed and recorded. Now, see, there's a lesson to be learned. Never accept a bribe from an Arab who asks you to talk into his camel's hump." Washington comedian Mark Russell told his D.C. audience: "The politicans should have known they were dealing with the FBI and not Arabian sheiks. Nobody wears a burnoose with wingtipped shoes."

During his 1980 Thanksgiving special "What Have We Got To Be Thankful For?," comedian Alan King did a take-off on the closed circuit films the FBI agents used to tape and eventually convict the

Congressmen. In King's skit, M*A*S*H star McLean Stevenson acts out the role of Congressman Hutton, who must appear at a Congressional inquiry. Hutton denies being involved with Arabs, but then we see a videotape which shows Hutton and an FBI agent posing as Sheik Mustafa. Wearing a robe and sunglasses and in bad need of a shave, the sheik sits and stares but never speaks.

Congressman Hutton offers the phony sheik a drink. A second FBI agent acts as the mute Mustafa's spokesman:

> Agent: Sheik Mustafa does not partake of liquor. It's against his religion.
> Hutton: Oh well, with a little taste of the sauce here, he can start a new religion.
> Agent: Sheik Mustafa is interested in making some very large purchases.
> Hutton: Tell him there's two Congressmen and a mayor for sale . . . What kind of investments did you wanna make?
> Agent: Real estate. He would like to buy Nevada. . . . Sheik Mustafa might one day seek asylum in the United States. He's having trouble at home.
> Hutton: Hey, who wouldn't with 37 wives? (He laughs.)
> Agent: He needs you to introduce a private bill in Congress to ensure his permanent residence in this country. Can you do it?

Hutton agrees and the videotape concludes by showing the Congressman accepting money. He pleads with the Investigating Committee: "OPEC has been rippin' us off on this oil deal and I thought it only patriotic to get some of that money back." Apparently, NBC's broadcast standards officials altered Hutton's line before airing the show. In *TV Guide*, the NBC promo stated, "The *Arabs* (not OPEC) took so much (money) from us, it's only patriotic to take some of it back."

King's ABSCAM skit gives the false impression that Arabs, not FBI agents are bribing Congressmen.

On the CBS Evening News one night, anchorman Walter Cronkite made the same mistake, referring to ABSCAM as a case of "alleged briberies by *Arab* interests." Cronkite's reference would have been accurate had he reported "alleged bribery by FBI men claiming to be Arabs." When a former *U.S. News and World Report* reporter wrote to Cronkite pointing out the error, the correspondent replied, "Good point."

Alan King follows the skit with a satirical "Middle East History Lesson." Here we learn comedian Danny Thomas is the "King of

Lebanon." "On the West Bank," King continues, "Begin is curtailing settlements and opting for condominiums." "Syria is busy keeping the peace in Lebanon," says King, "and they're doing a good job—Lebanon is in pieces." The comedian frowns when describing the clothes of Oman's Sultan Qaboos. "What the hell is he dressed up for? Oman's got eleven people and a goat." (Laughter.) King's writers obviously missed the 1979 *NBC White Paper* on oil and American power. Here, correspondent Garrick Utley stated that more than half the world's oil has to pass through the Strait of Hormuz and that "the guardian of the Strait of Hormuz is the Sultanate of Oman (Sultan Qaboos)." Utley correctly pointed out that "Oman and the United States have had diplomatic relations since the early 19th Century."

If our relations with Oman were not good and if the country aligned itself with the Soviets, we would probably experience an unparalleled energy crisis. The flow of oil through Oman's Strait of Hormuz, as correspondent Utley emphasized, is essential to the industrialized nations of the world.

Oman is the second largest state on the Arabian Peninsula and has a population of approximately one million people. It has over 500 elementary and secondary schools and special evening classes are held for adults wishing to learn to read and write. Muscat, Oman's capital, has several major hospitals, an international airport, and a work force that includes many women.

As with other Arabian Gulf States, there are numerous construction projects under way in Oman. Advanced water systems now help desert land become green. Oman's modernization program includes a desalination plant, a 650-mile coastal highway and a water port at Mutrah which will handle 1.5 million long-tons of cargo per year. Construction of additional schools, hospitals, hotels and homes is also under way.

Arab oil wealth and investment here has also provided a significant amount of joke fodder. This theme became popular in the mid-Seventies amidst the great gas shortage. A hit comedy-variety show of that era was *The Sonny and Cher Comedy Hour*. One *Sonny and Cher* show from that epoch featured a spoof that other comedy shows would later repeat with slight variations. In the skit, a group of enthusiastic all-American-type singers perform the uplifting favorite, "This Land is Your Land, This Land is My Land." The cameras captured them beaming with pride as they stood atop a large jigsaw map of the United States. Suddenly, out of the shadowy wings come Arabs. They do not join in the singing. Rather, they begin sneaking offstage, clutching selected states in their hands. The audience howled.

More accurate, entertaining programs are certainly possible. For example, television producers might consider co-producing variety shows with their counterparts in the Middle East. Numerous festivals take place in the summer in Arab lands. For twenty years, Lebanon's Baalbek Festival has provided an arena for impressive groups and artists, including the Pittsburgh and Cincinnati Symphonic Orchestras, the Royal Ballet with Dame Margot Fonteyn and Rudolf Nureyev.

Another cultural showcase of the region is Jordan's annual Jerash Festival. Against the historic backdrop of the 2,000-year-old city of Jerash, musicians, performers, artists and craftspersons from the Middle East and other nations gather together in a grand display of talent that attracts thousands of spectators.

American television viewers did not see these performances. Yet, such international festivals could be beamed by satellite to American homes, enabling U.S. citizens to see American and Arab talent performing side-by-side.

There is no reason why an Arab family could not be the subject of a situation comedy. The people in the Middle East take pride in close family ties and hospitality. On one visit to Beirut, I remember I was waiting for a bus on a hot afternoon as the mid-summer sun began to affect me. A nearby shopkeeper named "Goldfinger" sensed my discomfort and invited me into his store, which was much cooler than outdoors. He gave me a chair and we bent elbows over the counter drinking cold Pepsi for nearly an hour. I departed thanking Goldfinger for his kindness. Every time I'd thank him, he'd thank me. This thank you routine went on for so long I almost missed my bus. Goldfinger's door, like that of most everyone I know in the Middle East, is always open.

When I was on a visit to Cairo with my wife, we went to the city zoo, where we met an Egyptian couple and their son, who were also making the rounds. The boy was trying to manage an oversized multi-colored beach ball with his tiny hands. Suddenly, a brisk wind took the ball and guided it toward me. Before the ball could whiz past, I made a two-handed catch and returned it. The boy's parents thanked me and then asked us to join them for tea and refreshments. It was a cool day and a cup of sweet, hot Egyptian tea sounded fine. The young man told us he worked at the comptroller's office of the American University in Cairo while his wife was a part-time student and full-time housewife.

He said he enjoyed being with the Americans he met at the

university and liked the American TV programs which appeared on Egyptian television. But he was disturbed about how Arabs are portrayed in the West. Why are we always "bad people?" he asked. "Lack of exposure," I replied. Most television writers and producers don't know the people of the Middle East; their perceptions come primarily from old movies.

The *Sonny and Cher* show has been off the air for several years. But skits that highlight petrophobia remained. In 1980, the year after a gas shortage forced long waiting lines at American service stations, a *Bob Newhart* special picked up on the issue. Viewers of the special were first shown actual footage of the 1979 gas lines. Suddenly, the audience sees a grey Cadillac limousine pull up to the lines. The car is occupied by bearded Arabs wearing sunglasses. "Fill it up," one of the Arabs orders the attendants. They do so—not with gas in the tank, but bags of loot in the trunk. "More, more," says the Arab. When the trunk is at last overflowing, he smiles and says to the attendants, "Same time tomorrow." Following the loot-in-the-trunk skit, the camera cuts to the gas pumps. We see no posted prices. Instead, each pump has a sign that says, "Guess, Guess.".

Newhart's 1981 special depended on some of the same themes. In one segment, the comedian bemoans having to give up his Rolls-Royce. "It's over, baby," he says. "You're a guzzler. I just haven't got what it takes to turn you on anymore.... But *he* has," Newhart says, nodding toward an Arab in a headdress and robe who proceeds to hand him a check. The smiling Arab then cruises off in the Rolls. Newhart putters off on a moped.

Shows like *Sonny and Cher* and the *Bob Newhart* specials began as fairly traditional, light-hearted comedy skits. In recent years, however, comedy variety shows have grown more sophisticated. Most of these shows were intended to make people laugh. Now, many aim to make serious social statements under the veil of satire. NBC's hit show, *Saturday Night Live,* is a perfect case in point. But it is particularly disappointing to observe a show of that caliber slip into using the most demeaning stereotypes to portray a particular ethnic group. One *Saturday Night* segment was entitled "The Bel-Airabs" and was a take-off on the popular CBS series of the Sixties, *The Beverly Hillbillies.* In that show the hillbillies were hokey, naive, but nonetheless loveable country folk. I remember watching one *Hillbillies* program where Jed Clampett (Buddy Ebsen) chided an Arab about oil. The skit adhered to the stereotype but was not malicious. By contrast, the Bel-Airabs were stupid and unattractive, with crude manners.

The music from the theme song of the old *Hillbillies* show and the following lyrics introduce the segment:

> Come and listen to my story
> 'Bout a man named Abdul
> A poor Bedouin barely kept his family fed
> And then one day he was shootin' at some Jews
> And up through the sand came a bubblin' crude
> Oil, that is.
> Persian Perrier.
> Kuwait Kool-Aid.
> Saudi soda.

The story is about Abdul Assad who discovers oil on his land. Together with his son Mudhat, daughter Fatima and their granny, Abdul moves to Beverly Hills, arriving there on a camel. The first scene shows Mudhat painting red pubic hair on a nude statue outside their house. Mudhat makes it clear he enjoys women with red hair. But Granny, sliding down the banister in her *abaya,* insists that he change the color. Granny likes brunettes. Mudhat reluctantly agrees.

I wrote to NBC's Vice President of Program Resources, Bettye King Hoffmann, about the show. "I hope you will bear in mind that during the years this program has been on the air, just about everyone and everything has been satirized. If you have watched the program, you know that the satire and humor, while irreverent, is not malicious," she responded.

Arabs, like other minority groups, are fair game for satire. I agree, but skits need not be malicious to be in bad taste.

Like *Saturday Night Live,* several recent prime time comedies have taken the lead in dealing with some of the most sensitive issues of our day: abortion, rape, sexual morals, war and political corruption. Perhaps the most eminent television producer of situation comedies that dares to make controversial political and social statements is Norman Lear. During the 1970s, Lear made television history with controversial shows like *All in the Family, The Jeffersons, Maude, Mary Hartman, Mary Hartman* and *One Day at a Time.* He injected such sensitive issues as rape, abortion, vasectomy, Vietnam and Watergate into the world of situation comedy.

Speaking at a Children's Television Symposium, Lear emphasized the effectiveness of slipping public service messages into entertainment shows. "We have learned that more people will absorb information when it is couched in entertainment," Lear said then. "The higher the entertainment level of the show, the bigger the audience and the more successful the information," he added. Lear noted that a documentary on an important social issue will be only half as effective since many television viewers resent being lectured to.

In 1979, Lear was approached by the U.S. Department of Energy's Office of Conservation and Solar Lobby, a citizen's group, to convey messages on energy conservation in his shows. Later that year, *Archie Bunker's Place* (the spinoff series from *All in the Family*) included a segment which emphasized the importance of setting home thermostats at sixty-eight degrees. The viewing public may have received a positive message about energy conservation, but certainly they received quite a negative one about Arabs.

In that segment, Archie walks into his bar and sees everyone bundled up and shivering. He complains to his partner, Murray, and goes to raise the thermostat. Murray stops him, arguing that they must save energy. Obviously irritated, Archie relates a story he heard about a man who invented a pill which, when put in a gas tank with water, would give 500 miles to the gallon. But, Archie says, the oil companies got to the man and now, "The guy is living high in Saudi Arabia in a fourteen-room inflatable tent with seven wives he don't even have to look at."

In an early *All in the Family* episode, Archie berates a wishy-washy Arab laundromat owner. The "Ay-rab," as Archie calls him, cries when he doesn't get his way. The show opens with Archie rushing home and locking his door. He tells his wife Edith, "Don't go near that Ay-rab again unless you got a dirty camel to wash." Archie is angry because the clothes he took to the laundry are in shreds. "I'm gonna sue that Egyptian phony," he swears.

Archie's son-in-law Michael interrupts: "He's not an Egyptian. He's Syrian."

Growls Archie, "It's the same thing. They're born pirates, all of 'em."

In *All In The Family* we expect Archie to say these things. It's part of the character. He berates "Polacks," "Spades," and "Spics." But usually, Archie's ethnic slurs are challenged. In most episodes, Archie's prejudices are portrayed as self-damaging, and it is obvious that he misses out on much in life because of his racist behavior. In this show Archie fails to learn a lesson from his Arab diatribes.

It is interesting that one of the most popular programs on Israeli TV is a spinoff of *All in the Family*. The Israeli Archie continually berates Arabs. "Arabs stink," he declares in one episode.

The effect of the Israeli Archie's defamatory statements is difficult to assess. Some Israeli viewers, like their American counterparts, may perceive such comments as satire, an absurdity of prejudice. Others may see the character as their kind of guy, an affirmation of their own suspicions about a particular ethnic group. Can we expect those who view Archie as the latter to alter their views as long as he continues to nurture their prejudices?

Lear has been known to solicit comments about his programs before they are aired. He once withdrew a series about a black Congressman, called *Mr. Dugan,* after members of the Congressional Black Caucus protested about the material Lear intended to use. Lear later conceded, "We felt we were ineffectively presenting a black Congressman as a role model."

Lear says that he also consulted with the Jewish Anti-Defamation League, Catholic groups and the National Institute of Mental Health. Yet, he has never presented a humane Arab in any of his shows. I wrote and phoned producer Lear several times requesting an interview and received no response. I was puzzled. I had heard CBS official James Baerg state at a symposium at Georgetown University in 1979 (on The American Media and Arabs) that Lear has been "readily accessible" to those who have a grievance with his shows. Baerg said that if Lear does a show involving cardiopulmonary resuscitation, he has a doctor instruct the actors. If he does a show on gays, he asks advice of a representative of the gay community. Baerg said he believes Lear has been "one of the most responsive and sensitive people in Hollywood in this regard." He added that Lear cares about his image and cares about what he is presenting.

Lear did not grant me an interview, but I did meet with two of his associates, Alan Rafkin, executive producer of another Lear creation, *One Day at a Time,* and Virginia Carter, Lear's vice president of creative affairs. *One Day* has portrayed Arabs as fabulously wealthy and oblivious to social concerns. I mentioned the *One Day* episode to Carter. "Television," she said, "always generalizes and generalizations are always dangerous."

Generalizations abound in the *One Day* program that features an oil sheik accused of "buying up all the businesses in town." This sheik has "a palace in his homeland and a little place here—Rhode Island." When the Arab arrives in the U.S., protestors shout "Arabs go home." Angry demonstrators carry signs that read: "America is not for sale," and, "Arabs cannot have this country."

The series star, Ann Romano, must entertain the Arab because her boss wants the sheik to sign on with his public relations firm. Complains Ann, "What else do you want me to do, a belly dance?"

The sheik, a male chauvinist, will do business with a man but not with Ann Romano. Throughout the program, the writers stress that Arabs will not do business with women.

The Arabs put a high value on personal relationships in the conduct of their business matters. They warmly welcome the expertise of Mrs. Bonnie Pounds, the U.S. Director for the Saudi-Arabian-United States Joint Commission on Economic Cooperation.

For the past eight years Mrs. Pounds has been helping Saudis and Americans to understand one another better. Mrs. Pounds herself is a particularly good example of how differing cultures can interact successfully. "The Saudis know our culture is different and they respect it," says Mrs. Pounds. "I don't feel any awareness that they attach importance to the fact that I am a woman. We spend our time focusing on work problems. And of course my own actions are guided by a respect for *their* culture, too."

Meanwhile, back to the *One Day* segment. On learning Ann Romano will host the sheik, the feisty janitor Schneider says, "To make the guy feel more at home, I'll spread a little sand in the lobby." Schneider continually jokes about Arabs—he "doesn't want to be replaced by a desert nomad." Arab men call their women "ships of the desert—that's why they wear veils," says Schneider. He adds, "And Arab men make their wives walk five steps behind them. Except for World War II. Then they walked five steps in front of them." At one point the sheik is asked, "Have you heard of the ERA (Equal Rights Amendment)?" He replies, "The ERA? Is it for sale?"

Virginia Carter explained why the *One Day* program enhanced the myth that Arabs are buying up America. "Most of the people who create television programs live in Los Angeles. When they see real estate being purchased in Bel Air or Beverly Hills by Arabs, it is obviously bound to influence the way they write," she said.

"What we did with the *One Day* program, portraying an Arab buying up the country, I never gave it a second thought," said producer Alan Rafkin. "And that's because I'm not sensitive to everyone's stereotype." Rafkin believes that "most of the things people learn to love or hate or mistrust or adore, they get from television." He doesn't recall ever seeing a decent TV Arab, but recalled a familiar theme: "The Arab's from a fake country and he's the sheik of so-and-so. He's a terrific guy. But his father is evil. It's all *'Mission: Impossible'*."

"Or," said Virginia Carter, "He's the sheik of Araby folding his tent and slinking off into the night."

Carter explained that her associates make a living by doing controversial shows that deal with important social issues. "There are good people here," she said, "and when contrary points of view are available, our people tend to add it as grist to their mill and turn out a better TV show." Carter contends that Lear's company could certainly "do a show with an Arab character that got past the stereotype and into the real thing."

Rafkin told me that if CBS's *60 Minutes* telecast a show that examined Arab stereotypes, he would watch it. "I don't care how they hyped it. Arabs as you've never seen them. Arabs as real people. Arabs as whatever—I would watch." Added the producer, "We don't know anything about the Arab people."

Both Carter and Rafkin feel strongly about presenting a more balanced image. Carter said, "I'm still reeling at the idea that our shows might have contributed to the misrepresentation of the Arab character." I asked her why the stereotype exists. "Negative images do not result from malicious undercurrents of conscious hate or dislike," she said. "It's obviously rooted in misinformation or lack of information entirely."

Rafkin acknowledged that it is "safe" to stereotype Arabs because they lack a strong lobby—people who will speak up for them—in the television industry. "If producers show a hairdresser and he is flying around the room, the gays will be all over you," Rafkin explained. Rafkin said our discussion was in fact the first in which someone had raised with him the problem with Arab portrayals. "It's as rare as if someone came and said, 'I represent all the female dwarfs.' I swear to God, it's as rare as that."

The producer said he believes network broadcast standards officials could help bring about more accurate portrayals of various groups by looking for more than "dirty words and how many times you say hell" in a telecast. He suggested these officials "look for what people are portrayed as. Are we doing an injustice to people or are we setting a bad precedent, are we giving out information that is not necessarily true? That's what they should be looking for." Rafkin also said, "When I see a Jew portrayed as Shylock, I want to cry. So I know how an Arab feels when he's described as a killer or someone who can buy you anytime he wants."

One show which could provide limitless opportunities for a humane portrayal of Arabs is CBS's popular comedy about a truck-stop restaurant owner and his three zany waitresses, called *Alice*. The show

features the gifted Arab-American comedian Vic Tayback in the role of
Mel, the owner of the diner that is the show's setting.

Tayback's character is funny and loveable, but he is certainly not
portrayed as a character with Arab roots. The show's writers say they do
not want Mel to have a particular heritage. But why not? Why can't one
episode show Mel preparing an Arab meal consisting of *kusa mahshi*
(stuffed squash), *lahm kharouf* (roasted lamb) *kibbeh* (ground sirloin,
crushed wheat, onions and spices), *waraq inab* (rolled grape leaves filled
with meat and rice) and *hummos* (chick peas with a sesame seed paste)?

Mel's cousins could unexpectedly arrive from overseas, announce a
wedding party and declare Mel's diner the reception hall. During the
reception Mel and the diner gang could join the relatives in traditonal
dances. Musicians could play *ouds* (string instruments) and *derbukees*
(drums). Such an episode offers numerous recipes for humor. Vera, one
of the waitresses, could accidentally soak the grape leaves in vinegar, not
water. Mel could mistakenly punch holes in the squash so that all the
rice and meat fall out. Alice, another waitress, could forget to add the
sirloin to the *kibbeh*, leaving only balls of onion and crushed wheat.

The cousins would refuse to eat Mel's meal and his feelings would
be hurt. But when he explains how his gourmet nightmare took all
night to prepare, the cousins appreciate his efforts and request that he
substitute his Arab meal with some hamburgers, fries and apple pie.
Mel's pride soars. But with the reputed quality of Mel's food, the joke is
on everyone.

Instead of mining the rich supply of comedic material that exists in
Mel's Arab-American roots, the program all too often lapses into the
easy stereotypes. One episode, "Florence of Arabia," features the saucy
Flo in an encounter with Ben, an oil baron. The two meet at a checkout
lane at Quick Mart.

"Flo was buying a can of Spaghetti-Os and Ben was buying the Quick
Mart," Vera recounts.

"He's one of those Arabs who's coming over here to buy up the whole
country," Alice says.

"He had a roll of bills with pictures of presidents I never even seen," Flo
exclaims.

Ben, who wears a headdress with a "cheap" $500 suit, wants to take
Flo, Mel, Vera and Alice to his homeland in his modest 747 jet. Yet, in
the states, he quibbles over the price of gas.

Ben: I had a terrible experience in the gas station across the street.

Flo: What happened, Benji?

Ben: I filled up my tank. Oh my goodness, I don't know how you can afford those prices.

(In reality, as of December, 1981, some Arabs were paying more for gasoline than Americans. In Jordan, the price was $2.20 a gallon; in Syria and Lebanon, $1.50; in North Yemen it was $2.05 and in Morocco, $2.35.)

Ben tells Flo of the familiar Arab saying, "May the warmth of the setting sun heat the basement of your heart." He says his father coined the phrase "right after he imposed the oil embargo." Ben wants to make Flo his fourth wife because in his country, "red hair is considered to be hot stuff." He tells Alice that all of his brothers have four wives and that he will be merely catching up with them.

Alice: Kind of like a poker game, huh? Four of a kind.

Ben: Oh, no, they are not of a kind. They have four distinct personalities. They all have what you call 'their own thing.' When I wish to dance, I call on Yasmin. She is lithe of body and little of mind. When I am in the mood for music, I call on Fatima. She has the voice of a nightingale . . . and is little of mind. When I am in the mood for love, I call for Shanaz. She is of ample body . . .

Alice and Ben (together): And little of mind.

Later, Flo asks Alice: You mean I'm going to be part of a harem?

Alice: They don't divorce in the shadow of the pyramids, they just put another bed in the tent. . . . You're number four. The new anchor lady on the relay team.

At an Arab restaurant, Flo decides to ask Ben pointedly if he indeed has a harem.

Ben: My goodness no. It would be immodest of me to call three wives a harem.

Flo abruptly departs, but not before she throws her $100,000 ring into a soup bowl and says, "Ben, kiss my couscous."

In Burbank, I met with *Alice* producers Bob Carroll, Jr., and Madelyn Davis, to discuss the "Florence" episode and television stereotyping in general. Carroll told me that "stereotypes take a long time to wither away." Both producers said they had never seen humane or heroic Arab characters on television. This situation exists, they said, despite the fact that TV stereotyping "is not the 'in' thing to do .... It's not right to talk about fat people," Davis said. "Or scrawny or flat-chested (people)," Carroll added. "We don't like that on our shows. People make jokes about Vera. No breasts. And we say no."

I explained to the producers that viewers often see their favorite TV stars ridicule anything Arab—from fillies to fashion to food. Bing Crosby's daughter, Mary Frances, told Merv Griffin in a 1983 program that she was fond of her Arabian fillies. "We lie down together and sleep at night," she said. Griffin then equated Arabian horses with Arab people. "If you lie down with *Arabs*, (you) get up with fleas." Laughter from the audience and the interview ended.

Joan Rivers is often a guest host on *The Tonight Show*. She's usually very funny. But she wasn't very soul-searching one particular night. Concerning Arab fashions, she told viewers. "I can never tell if it's the wife or the husband because they're all in bedsheets."

Bob Hope, in his 1982 *Pink Panther/Thanksgiving Special*, tells viewers: "Not everyone in Beverly Hills has a turkey. The Arabs sacrifice a goat."

In *TV's Bloopers & Practical Jokes*, Phyllis Diller is wooed by a wealthy Arab who wants her for his harem. After checking Phyllis's teeth for cavities, the potentate overwhelms her with gifts, including a cute baby goat. "Good meat," says the Arab. The pet is to be the entree for supper.

In a *Hart to Hart* episode, the Harts grimace when they see their evening meal—"dried camel eggs."

When Mork prepares a Moroccan meal for Mindy in a *Mork and Mindy Show,*, he insists they eat with their fingers. First, they wash their hands in dishwashing liquid. "Feet next," chuckles Mork. Silverware is a no-no because "all the silverware in Morocco is used to break out of prisons." When Mindy gags on the food, Mork sighs, "It's so hard to get fresh camel lips in Boulder."

Viewers see unappetizing Arab cuisine and caricatures of Arabs wallowing in money and oil in many shows, including *WKRP in Cincinnati, Love Boat, Whodunnit?* and *Harper Valley P.T. A.* Arabs are heard boasting, "Look at me, I'm a sheik; people think I'm rich." And we see them sucking scraps from their fingers, losing harem maidens "in a poker game," giving away Rolls-Royces and "buying Palm Springs."

An Arab who gets high on crude, Omar the Oil-glut-Maniac, appears in an episode of ABC's 1983 summer series *The 1/2 Hour*

Comedy Show. Omar boasts, "I've got enough black gold to fill the Red Sea and I can't get rid of it. Why not put a little crude in your food?" he asks the belly dancers.

Omar demonstrates to viewers the exotic uses of oil: over pancakes and ice cream, as their hair tonic and hand lotion. "Oil is great at parties," says Omar. "You can massage your friends, or boil your enemies." Omar begins massaging dolls—first a blond Barbie, then Ken. Suddenly he tosses Ken into a boiling pot. "Ken, you stole one of my camels. You must die," chuckles Omar.

Condo, a series designed to "throw some light on a few of our prejudices," enhances prejudices. In one episode, James needs thousands to open a "Top Burger" franchise. He asks his friend Jesse, "Where do all the millionaires come from?" Replies Jesse, "Saudi Arabia. They come over here and buy up everything."

The image of the profligate is also used for the main character in segments of the *Trapper John, M.D.* and *Benson* series. In *Benson* a haughty Sheik Mameed with two insensible bodyguards, plans to sink $600 million into America's economy. "I am pleasured to meet you, Du Boo," he tells Benson. The sheik makes three demands. One, Kraus must join his desert harem—"no woman, no building." Two, his "ugly, ugly" arabesque building design, which resembles "a used wedding cake," must be accepted. And three, whatever Mameed asks for, Mameed gets.

At first, Benson and Kraus play along with the sheik's insulting behavior—they are reluctant to jeopardize the negotiation. But their behavior quickly changes when the "scum of Araby with bats in his *falafel*" deliberately smashes Benson's car to smithereens. The sheik also refuses to pay for damages, claiming diplomatic immunity.

When Mameed orders Benson to "Get me that woman" or "I'll have you fired," the sheik gets his comeuppance. Benson calls him a "dummy." Kraus calls him a "birdbrain" and a "dimestore Valentino." She tells this "Ali Baba and the fifty hands" to "take the camel he rode in on" and beat it.

"The Surrogate," a *Trapper John, M.D.* comedy written by producer Don Brinkley, shows another bumbling sheik. This one treats his daughter as a negotiated object. The Arab revels in an elaborate hospital room, complete with a tubby belly dancer and musicians. The decorative brocades and tentlike drapery arrangement imply that he can't get along in another country without stereotypical luxuries.

Gonzo arrives to thank the sheik for a half-million dollar donation to the hospital fund. It's a "pittance," said the Arab. "I'd like to give you something more personal. Something you'd enjoy having. A harem, perhaps? Your own hospital? The state of Pennsylvania?"

For Gonzo, the hospital donation is sufficient. On entering his trailer, however, he discovers an unexpected surprise—the sheik's daughter Aliya, who is "dressed in a slinky, skimpy harem costume, decorated with tiny silver bells."

Consider this excerpt:

Aliya: My father, the sheik, has sent me here. I am yours.
Gonzo: My what?
Aliya: Your wife, maid servant, slave. Whatever you wish. My father has given me to you as a gift.
Gonzo: That's one hell of a gift. Don't you have anything to say about it?
Aliya: Your will is my will. (She begins to remove Gonzo's clothes.)
Gonzo: C'mon. I'm taking you back.
Aliya: No! My father would be highly insulted.
Gonzo: Aren't *you* insulted by this kind of treatment?
Aliya: You don't know father. He's capable of terrible things.

Gonzo tells Aliya: "Catch the ten o'clock camel and go home." "My father," says Aliya, is "a product of another world. He's still living in another time. Any new ideas can be very painful to him." But if Aliya refuses to marry Gonzo, she may be banished to the loneliness of her homeland. Over there she would be given the task of "sweeping up camel dung," or "building a pipeline."

When Gonzo finds out that Aliya loves another man, Herbie, a nutritionist, he confronts the sheik: "She'll never be happy as my wife. I'm not the man she loves." Replies the sheik, "That doesn't matter." Shocked, Gonzo asks, "Your daughter's happiness doesn't matter? A father's first responsibility is the happiness and security of his family; isn't that so?"

Trapped by Gonzo's logic, the sheik offers his blessings to Aliya and Herbie, "overlooking centuries of tradition and protocol." Smiling, he and two "gigantic Arab bodyguards," whom Gonzo calls "goons," depart in an oversized Cadillac.

In Los Angeles, I met with producers Frank Glicksman and Don Brinkley. Brinkley took issue with my criticism of the sheik's giveaway daughter. "Understand the circumstances under which he gave his daughter away," he said. "The sheik wanted Gonzo for his son. He admired, respected and loved him." "Why did Aliya wait for Gonzo in the trailer dressed as a belly dancer?" I asked. "It's just theatrical—a fun thing," said Brinkley.

Brinkley saw nothing wrong with showing the sheik as wanting to buy "property" in America. "You should see Beverly Hills," he said. "Are you saying that because of what happens in Beverly Hills, the Arabs are buying up the country?" I asked. "Only a small chunk of it," said the producer.

At this point Glicksman interrupted saying, "Arabs are rarely portrayed as good guys. I've never seen them portrayed as anything but heavies in melodrama. That, I feel, is unfair."

Glicksman then asked me, "Jack, how did you—I'd be interested to know how you, a Jew...." "I'm not. My parents came from Lebanon," I said. Jokingly, Glicksman said he could now boast that "some of my best friends are Arabs." As the interview concluded, Brinkley told me, "I think you have a valid argument. I really do. The depiction of the Arab on television is generally horrendous."

Producers of television shows have a responsibility to entertain viewers, without offending them, to portray ethnic and minority groups without demeaning them. Opportunities for positive images obviously exist. For example, in one *Trapper John, M.D.* program the producers show Trapper falling in love with a beautiful Greek woman. We see the doctor adopting Greek customs and culture. The program concludes with a freeze-frame of a smiling Trapper doing a traditional Greek dance.

Television's coterie of talented writers and producers might consider providing more comedy shows in which Arabs are depicted, not as objects to be mocked, but as people to be respected—with feelings, weaknesses, strengths and a sense of humor.

Death of a Princess

In May 1980 the Public Broadcasting System (PBS) televised the American and British production *Death of a Princess* in the United States. *Princess* is a dramatized version about the real-life public execution of a beautiful Saudi princess and her lower-class lover for adultery. The show employed a relatively new concept of programming, the "docudrama," which some critics refer to as "docufiction." Producers discourage misleading statements and blatant distortions in their documentaries. But in public and commercial network docudramas, few ground rules exist. The danger is obvious: viewers may perceive fiction as fact. How can they discern which is truth?

Actress Elizabeth Taylor, for example, on learning that ABC-TV dropped plans for a 1983 docudrama based on her life, was "extremely gratified." Said Ms. Taylor: "I have long believed that the so-called docudrama misleads the public by combining fact and fiction in such a way that the two are indistinguishable."

Like other network programs, including newscasts, the process of making *Princess* and other docudramas requires value judgments: the judgment of the cinematographer, producer and director as to what to film or not to film; of the writer and editor as to what information to leave in or to take out; and of the performers as to what gestures and voice inflection to use. Although docudramas like *Princess* focus on some factual incidents, those events occur within fictional frameworks. Conversely, other docudramas may use factual contexts to insert fictional characters and incidents. The promotion of *Princess* was such that viewers could have perceived it as the absolute truth.

The purpose of my analysis of *Princess* is twofold. First, to offer some insights concerning the inherent risks of the docudrama format. Secondly, to discuss both old and new stereotypes appearing in the

71

program. We also need to look at the 100-minute film in terms of broadcast standards and ethics. Rarely has a single television program caused so much controversy prior to telecast. The questions were raised: how vulnerable is television to corporate influence and the pressures of petro-powers? To what extent is television covered by the First Amendment?

British authors Anthony Thomas and David Fanning wrote and produced *Princess*. They had been intrigued by the reported public execution in 1977 of Princess Misha'al and her lover which the Saudis did not deny. Thomas set out to ascertain what actually happened. On April 9, 1980, Thomas' version of the execution was first broadcast on ITV, the British independent network. The following day, London's *Evening Standard* reported that the Saudis were attempting to prevent freedom of expression through bribery and censorship. The newspaper featured a photograph of Saudi Arabia's ruler, King Khaled, on the front page and above it the headline:

SAUDI KINGS £5M TO BUY SILENCE

The *Standard*'s TV correspondent Sue Summers claimed that "King Khaled of Saudi Arabia made a £5,000,000 offer for the controversial ITV film *Death of a Princess* to stop it from being screened." Summers did not say who gave her this information.

Within 24 hours the Associated Press had embellished the story. Many newspapers and magazines in Europe and in the United States published the AP report, which was based on unnamed "sources connected with the film." A subsequent story that appeared in *The Daily Telegraph* two days later, on April 11, categorically denied the bribe.

Charles Denton, ITV's program controller, told a *Telegraph* reporter: "I have heard rumors about money being offered, one sum mentioned was £5 million, another which was rumored in America was £10 million, so you can almost name your own sum." Denton added: "It is, of course, a good story and a lot of hot air is being generated by it. But I have absolutely no knowledge of any offer of money being made at all and I would be astonished if one was made without me knowing it."

Denton's denial, however, did not receive local, national or international coverage. Most commentators and cartoonists ignored Denton's comments and accepted instead the Summers' bribery story as fact. London's newspapers had a field day with it. One cartoon showed an oversized Saudi and underneath his scowling face, the caption: "Big Arab is Watching You." Another cartoon pictured an executioner preparing to behead an Arab woman; she was caught "watching the telly," the cartoon said. Several of London's newspapers hyped *Princess* with sensational headlines—"Tales of Arabian Savagery," "How a Princess Died in the Dust," and "The Sands of Mystery."

The Saudis reacted strongly following the telecast. The royal family felt it was being attacked. The Saudis recalled their ambassador from Great Britain and asked the British envoy to leave Saudi Arabia. British Foreign Secretary Lord Carrington sent a message of "profound regret" to Saudi Prince Saud about "any offense the film may have caused." Carrington's actions met with a mixed response from Parliament. One Labor Party official said that the film was "an overtly political attack in the guise of entertainment." Another, however, complained: "We are getting on our knees to these sadistic types who obviously do not like the truth."

The airing of *Princess* threatened, at least temporarily, Saudi-British relations. The jobs of some 30,000 Britons in Saudi Arabia were at stake and there was a possibility that a $2 billion annual trade agreement between the countries would be jeopardized. Newspapers such as *Saudi News* defended the government's diplomatic action against Britain and warned that they would take similar steps against nations "which may indulge in abuse against the Kingdom, the Royal Family and Islamic tradition."

The Saudis hoped the diplomatic stir in Britain would discourage other countries from telecasting *Princess*. But most countries ignored Saudi requests to ban it. In Cannes, primarily because the British press gave *Princess* such advance publicity, distributors sold the drama to 25 countries "at five times the normal price," according to London's *Evening Standard*. Rumors of bribery accomplished one thing—plenty of free publicity for the film and its owners. The Saudi effort to suppress *Princess* succeeded only in gaining a far larger audience for the film. It became the most controversial television program of 1980.

Shortly after the London showing, *Princess* reached the United States. Producers David Fanning and Anthony Thomas appeared on national television, including *Today* and *Good Morning, America*, to discuss their film. Prior to his *Today* appearance on NBC, Fanning said he was "surprised and very disappointed by the Royal Family's reaction to *Princess*. I think it's a very sympathetic view of the Arab world; a careful attempt to show another side of the Arab world," he said.

The talk shows, however, showed the most tantalizing excerpts of the program. "Let's look at the scene where the boyfriend is beheaded," said Tom Brokaw, formerly of *Today*, before his interview with Fanning. "This is a fictionalized account of something that happened.

Right?" Brokaw asked. Fanning did not answer. For some reason Brokaw did not pursue the question. Why did the producer tactfully avoid that admission?

On ABC, David Hartman's interviews on *Good Morning, America* were more balanced. Unlike *Today*'s presentation, ABC did not show a film clip of the beheading to spark viewer interest. The *Good Morning, America* show included Fouad Ajami, Director of Middle East Studies at Johns Hopkins University's School of Advanced International Studies, as well as Anthony Thomas. Ajami accused Thomas of making "a lot of Arabs in the movie into caricatures." He added: "Some of the women displayed in the film are grotesque representations of Arab women. . . . I think that's really from Mr. Thomas' own thoughts." Ajami also emphasized that "the traffic of images is a one-way street and the West is always judging." Ajami, however, said he felt the American Public Broadcasting System had every right to air the program.

"This is not a caricature of the Arab image . . . . The Arabs are articulate, intelligent, warm and sympathetic," Thomas told Ajami. He quoted some Arabs as saying, "Thank God, you got away from the [Arab] cartoon stereotypes and got to this."

Hartman, like Brokaw, asked a critical question that remained unanswered. "Do you have evidence that this story is actually a true story?" Thomas merely answered, "Oh yes, I know the girl died."

Then he went on to say the show "is about the trauma, if you like, of being an Arab in 1978 . . . . I did something like 300 hours of interviews with Arab friends, journalists, and contacts. The film is not my perspective. It is an Arab perspective." Hartman challenged this statement, pointing out that the selection of material and the editing of a movie of any kind can make a statement of its own.

Two of his film's performers severely criticized Thomas' remarks—Egyptian actors Samir Sabri and Tahany Rashed. Both of them told NBC reporter James Compton that the producers misled them about the film's statement. They said they expected to see a different film about the Arab world, a film offsetting, not enhancing stereotypes. Instead, it turned out to be "a deliberate attack on the royal family," said Sabri. Rashed said Thomas missed "a marvelous opportunity to bring across the real issues of the Arab world to a Western audience. If I were a Western viewer," she said, "I would come away feeling personally revolted, disgusted, very superior and more smug in my feelings of resentment for Saudi Arabia."

Promoters, meanwhile, billed *Princess* as "a true story," "a true investigation," and "a factual account" of an Arabian princess who died for love. Editorial pages and network reporters and personalities continually spoke of "Saudi pressure." Some reporters said the Saudis might cut off oil to the United States if it aired *Princess*. Other stories said the show would go on—oil or no oil.

At one point, David Hartman reported that "The United States State Department received a request from the Saudis to keep this movie off television." In the New York *Times*, Bernard Gwertzman reported: "This was the first time that the State Department had been asked by a government to intercede in advance of a televised film . . . . In the past, protests had been made after the movies had been shown."

Today's Tom Brokaw commented: "The Saudi Arabians don't like the film and they started a campaign to discourage its airing here." Brokaw added that the Saudis are attempting "to dictate to us what we can see and cannot see about their country."

But was there actually an attempt at "censorship" by the Saudis? Saudi Ambassador to Washington, Sheik Faisal Alhegelan, did write a letter to Acting Secretary of State Warren M. Christopher. But he did not ask Christopher "to keep this movie off television," as David Hartman said. There was no threat of an oil embargo. His letter stated, in part: "We recognize your constitutional guarantees of freedom of speech and expression and it is not my purpose to suggest any infringement . . . . However, we feel you and other responsible officials of your government would want to know our concern and the reasons, therefore, before the film is shown." The Ambassador explained, "The film shows a completely false picture of the life, religion, customs and traditions of Saudi Arabia. It also, in many ways, is disparaging to the Moslem religion." He added, "The film is therefore offensive not only to Saudi Arabia but to the entire Islamic world."

Ambassador Alhegelan said he believed it was not ethical to promote a fictitious drama as "factual," fearing viewers would accept the film as "the way it is today in Saudi Arabia." He requested that "the Public Broadcasting System or the news media *determine for themselves* what the fictitious items and distortions are" and "not report them to the American public as fact."

The Ambassador's letter, wrote TV-critic Ron Alridge in the Chicago *Tribune*, "hardly suggests the Saudis are bracing for diplomatic warfare. It simply asks for good journalism." Alridge maintained the problem with the program was that "the reporter [Anthony Thomas] wasn't able to learn the truth. Instead he emerged with a confusing collection of rumors, gossip and contradictory stories." Added Alridge, "What the show needs is a clear, up-front explanation that it is drama, not documentary."

Secretary Christopher passed on the Ambassador's letter, along with his own, to PBS President Leonard Grossman. Christopher's letter to Grossman said that the United States government would not attempt to exercise any power of censorship: "We have no doubt you will give appropriate consideration to the sensitive religious and cultural issues involved, and assure that viewers are given a full and balanced presentation," it said. Perhaps Christopher was reminding Grossman not only of Saudi concern but of the Public Broadcasting Act of 1967 and Public Law 90-129, which calls for "adherence to objectivity in all programs or series of programs of a controversial nature." The 1967 law prohibits the Public Broadcasting System from accepting any program "the purpose of which, in the opinion of (PBS) is to ridicule, attack, or otherwise misrepresent any individual or group on the basis of race, color, national origin or sex . . . ."

Media attention toward the film intensified when Mobil Oil, which contributes millions of dollars to public television each year, produced an ad, "The New Fairy Tale," which suggested that PBS review its decision to air *Princess.* That led to speculation in the media; would the "Petroleum" Broadcasting System cancel the show? But Mobil's spokesman, Bryant Mason, stated that his corporation "had not contacted PBS or any public television stations about the film." As for the Saudis, Mason issued a press release stating they "had not communicated with Mobil" about *Princess.*

Only 16 of PBS's more than 200 stations decided against airing the film. Obviously, the pre-broadcast furor had generated tremendous publicity and therefore interest in the program. *Broadcasting* magazine reported that *Princess* attracted one of the largest audiences in the history of PBS (it was the fourth most-watched program. The three top-rated PBS shows are a 1975 *National Geographic* special, "The Incredible Machine," and two live specials from *The Grand Ole Opry,* telecast in 1979 and 1980). *Princess* received "the highest overnight ratings since PBS started keeping tests."

The film itself contains impressive cinematography which transports the viewer to an Arab world of mystery, a montage of camels and Cadillacs, complete with shadowy figures lurking among the facades of ultramodern skyscrapers.

The drama begins with stark, emotionally contrasting scenes. In the desert, a motionless camel poses in front of a Bedouin's tent. A red jeep leading a caravan of cars speeds recklessly onward, blowing up the desert dust. The old and new Arabia.

The jeep pulls into a small town. It passes men praying inside a mosque, a veiled woman in black walking slowly down a narrow street. Then it stops in a parking lot covered with freshly dumped sand. Suddenly a bound woman is thrust from the back of a truck onto the sand. The caravan's occupants emerge and a shot rings out. The camera freezes on a British worker who allegedly witnessed the execution. Simultaneously the title appears: *Death of a Princess*.

The show follows the path of fictional journalist Christopher Ryder as he tries to piece together the fate of Princess Misha'al. His first scrap of information comes from the British worker who witnessed the killing. The early scenes show men praying in a mosque, then scurrying to watch the lover's execution. The British worker says of the onlookers, "It's funny, isn't it? Straight out of church and off to see the bloke get chopped." Images appear on the screen that are never explained: the mysterious veiled woman, the chanting man in the mosque, men who embrace and kiss one another on the street. It is common custom for Arab men to greet one another this way. But without explanation, Western viewers could perceive this as a sign of homosexuality.

The British worker offers Ryder this insight into Saudi Arabia: he calls it "a smelly tip with rubbish all over the place." With that in mind, Ryder sets out to discover the truth about the princess' death with an Arab associate, Marwan Shaheen. Shaheen tells Ryder the princess' death is more than a story about an individual. It is "the story of 200 million people ... the whole Arab predicament." But is it?

The *Princess* producers portray the Islamic religion as a barbaric system. In his book *Militant Islam* Godfrey H. Jansen, an expert on Islam, says most Westerners perceive Islam, a faith of 800 million people, as consisting of "strange bearded men with burning eyes, hieratic figures with robes and turbans, blood dripping from the amputated hands and from the striped backs of malefactors, and piles of stones barely concealing the battered bodies of adulterous couples."

"Odious Western images of Mohammed and of Islam have a long and embarrassingly honorable lineage," writes Harvey Cox of the Harvard University Divinity School in an article for *Atlantic*. Dante reserved a special place in hell for Mohammed. "The prophet's punishment," says Cox, "was to be eternally chopped in half from his chin to his anus," spilling entrails and excrement at the door of Satan's stronghold." Little has changed in 600 years. The Italian poet's unflattering portrait remains. "The image of the Moslem," writes Cox, "is still linked with revolting violence, distorted doctrine, a dangerous economic idea and the tantalizing tint of illicit sensuality."

Islam stresses equality, not antagonism, between races and nations. "Islam means submission of one's will to the will of God," writes

Jerrold E. Fix, Mid-West representative of the Middle East Institute in Washington D.C.. In *The Traditional World of Islam,* Fix explains that the Islamic mosque, like the Christian church, "is also a peaceful oasis for calm prayer and meditation." He describes an old man preparing for prayer in the desert, as generations have done before him. "As there is no water available for him to wash, as one must always do before praying," notes Fix, "he uses sand." The man's actions are slow and deliberate, and he clearly understands and respects their vital significance. Humble as his material circumstances clearly are, he is a picture of quiet dignity; it is on such dignity that true civilization rests, according to the Islamic belief. Regrettably, this type of dignity is absent from *Princess.*

Following his interview with the British worker, Ryder goes to Beirut, Lebanon where the Princess had spent some time. There he witnesses the Beirut of the late 70s—a scorched hell of needless suffering.

Ryder concentrates temporarily on the plight of the Palestinian refugees. One Palestinian family explains how it feels to be deprived of a homeland. He views the clashing images of Beirut: by day, a destroyed hotel with sun-bathers at the beach, a cosmopolis on the verge of collapse; by night, confusion and fear. An armed guard escorts him one night to a friend's home. There, he sees old men and women huddle together while children play with firecrackers. They are here because "it feels safe," explains Ryder's friend. "The ordinary Lebanese, they are the victims. They have to bear the burden of everyone else's fight .... I love my country, but it's finished," he sighs. Machine-gun fire and firecrackers (who knows which?) are heard in the background throughout their conversations.

Later back in Ryder's hotel the generator breaks down and he must use candlelight. He sees immobile faces on the hotel balconies listening to garbled voices on the radio. The static distortion reflects human frailty in a moving scene that may be one of television's best commentaries on the Lebanese crisis.

Ryder's attempts to find the Princess' whereabouts in Beirut consistently fail. Then one man tells him that the Princess appeared regularly "at Tramps Discotheque, dancing, dancing." The film's conflict begins unraveling: youth rebellion against a strict, authoritarian moral/religious legal code.

Ryder returns to London and meets with the Princess' nanny, Elsa Gruber. (The actual nanny had nothing to do with *Princess*; on London TV she said the film was fiction.) She tells Ryder that living in the palace is like life in prison for a woman. The princesses are "caged up in those palaces" and the only exercise they have, she says, is "hopefully making love." As for prayer, "in our palaces, praying was for the servants," said Gruber.

The director supports Gruber's versions of palace life with striking visuals. We see obese Arab women singing traditional songs and playing musical instruments at the palace. But we see Princess Misha'al smoking and playing Western pop music. We see her as a free spirit defying both her grandfather, Prince Mohammad, and the boredom which fetters her and her friends.

The actor playing Prince Mohammed appears only once, in a palace scene. Described by Gruber as "one of the original Arab playboys," we see the Prince entering from the shadows smiling, playing with youngsters, looking almost holy. We also see a warm and tender moment when he and the Princess share thoughts. Yet, earlier in the film, one performer described Prince Mohammed to Ryder as "a typically reactionary Prince, one of those who rode out of the desert, sword in hand ... who had the balls to take the life of his favorite granddaughter (Princess Misha'al), in order to save his image publicly."

Ryder decides to visit Saudi Arabia and find out for himself about the Prince. The scenes of Arabia are impressive, focusing on the old and the new—a donkey pulling a cart, streams of autos jammed at intersections, a camel in a bazaar, skyscrapers and workers hauling bricks as they did in 1900. He soon finds the country is only modern to an extent. The phones don't work. The telephone operators tell Ryder to "take a taxi—it's faster." In the Saudi capital, he meets with a British diplomat who says the Princess is alive and that "the old Prince paid a Bedouin family a vast sum for one of their daughters. She substituted for the Princess." His statement implies that Arab parents are not only backward but also mercenary and heartless. As for Prince Mohammed's involvement, the diplomat whispers, "They'll do anything to save the old bugger's honor." He advises Ryder to be careful: "I wouldn't want to have to come to your rescue."

Ryder goes to interview one Madame Quataajy, the owner of a boutique the Princess used to frequent. Mme. Quataajy explains that "strong punishments make our country safe," and the Princess "had to be sacrificed." Ryder fails to ascertain how, why or by whom. The viewer is in the same boat. Far into the drama, we are completely bewildered as to Princess Misha'al's fate.

Ryder gets little more information from the Saudi Ministry of Information. There, the information minister, complete with several gold teeth and shaded glasses, warns Ryder that his country "has invested heavily in the West," and he'd do well to lay off the *Princess's* story. The implication is that the minister of information is also the government's chief censor, a man without scruples.

A breakthrough comes when Ryder meets a mysterious woman named Emira who supposedly knows the truth about the Princess' death. Emira acts as a know-it-all mystic and describes for Ryder the endless boredom of one divorced princess whose greatest pleasure was to go out in her chauffeured car to the International Hotel at night, not for sex, but for a hamburger. "She sits there in the car, in the dark, for hours, just to watch people coming in and out," sighs the Emira.

Ryder asks about rights and privileges of a princess. "Sex," says the Emira, "to relieve the boredom. These princesses live the most intricate and busy sex lives ... quick liaisons. Sometimes cruel, always dangerous."

The camera shifts from her dimly-lit face to a desert highway. She speaks of veiled women as "the predators." We see an isolated desert road and black-veiled women in the backs of limousines. "There's always ways of finding a man," explains Emira. At night, sitting in their darkened cars, women watch men perform the traditional sword dance near a burning fire. The men know the women are judging them. The dazzling firelight suggests the intensity of desperate affairs. Women in black. Cruising. Choosing men in the heat of the Arabian desert.

Former U.S. Ambassador to Saudi Arabia James Aikens said these scenes were the most offensive to the Saudi government. "It's not true. It just doesn't happen. I've served in the area off and on for some thirty years. There are no secrets in Arabia." *Time*'s Beirut bureau chief, William Stewart, agreed: "In Saudi Arabia, of all places, such a scene is unimaginable .... No doubt the thought of sexual dalliance must occur to some princesses ... but that does not make Jeddah or Riyadh an Arabian nights version of *La Dolce Vita*." Such dramatizations make *Princess* dangerous and confusing to the uninformed viewer.

Throughout the film, producers Thomas and Fanning give us conflicting stories about the Princess' fate. They conclude the drama, however, by strongly suggesting that Prince Mohammed and Saudi Arabia's autocratic regime are responsible for her execution. "They implement tribal law, not Islamic justice," one young woman student tells Ryder. "This isn't a Moslem country. These people pervert Islam. They use Islam. They scare people to death with their barbarous punishments. This is not the way with Islam," she says.

Her ramblings—everything's-wrong-with-the-Saudis—illustrate the producers' bias. Their vision of the Saudi people is distorted. But what disturbs one most is why such dialogue is permitted to appear under the guise of truth.

At one point in *Princess*, Christopher Ryder exclaims: "I wish I had some facts—some simple facts." That, indeed, is something the intelligent viewer might also desire. What the viewer gets instead is both unsatisfying and unethical manipulation of real events into fictional drama.

Producers Anthony Thomas and David Fanning employed a host of notable Arab performers and traveled to Saudi Arabia, Lebanon and Egypt. Most of their research and compelling cinematography took place in Egypt, not Saudi Arabia. They had hoped to discover who killed the Princess; they also intended to reveal the "how" and "why" of the execution and to share their findings with an audience.

The problem facing Thomas and Fanning was how to ascertain the "truth" about the Princess and her lover. Thomas researched his story for nine months, conducting nearly 300 hours of interviews. But the interviews offered only conflicting interpretations. They also failed in their efforts to meet with those closely associated with the tragedy. "Only two of the interviewees actually knew the Princess," noted reporter Nancy Banks-Smith in *The Guardian*. Thomas, for instance, never saw the Princess' grandfather, Prince Mohammed, the oldest surviving son of Ibn Saud, Saudi Arabia's founder, and one of the most influential figures in the royal family.

The well-known British author Penelope Mortimer, who accompanied producer Thomas on his trip to Saudi Arabia, said: "Every interview and every character in the film is fabricated." The revelation of the domestic lives of the Saudi princesses—man-hunting in the desert, having *rendezvous* in boutiques—was based entirely on the statements of one person. Mortimer, involved with the project for nearly a year, was present at most of the interviews. "No real effort was made to check on such information. Rumor and opinion somehow came to be presented as fact," she said.

Truth is often the first casualty when a program such as *Princess* is dramatized and labeled docudrama. The danger of the docudrama is that viewers may perceive a program as completely factual—unlike a fictionalized entertainment show. It is practically impossible for viewers to separate fact from fiction when complex issues are presented.

But docudramas reflect advocacy journalism, conveying the point of view of the producer, the writer or the network. *Princess* as pseudo-drama is show biz, pure and simple.

Just hours before *Princess* was telecast, David Brinkley, on the NBC *Nightly News*, said: "The Saudi Ambassador to Washington says he has no objection to the program, only to the fact that it's labeled a docudrama. A mixture of fact and fiction. He says about five percent is fact and the rest is fiction, and he doubts if the audience will know which is which. So, he finds it deceptive. A TV critic who has seen it finds it a terrible bore ... poor journalism and poor drama."

Fouad Ajami has said: "To really come to terms with this film there are two traps we must avoid. The first would be to use the film as a weapon with which to indict an entire civilization, as a way of proving some point or another, feeling smug about our own world here and contemptuous of theirs."

Continued Ajami, "The second trap would be to say that its showing is improper, that it is propagandistic, that it is inspired by some conspiracy. Both are easy ways out ... both traps do nothing to enhance our desperate search for ways that make it easier for us to understand one another and to share this increasingly troubled and precarious world."

Death of a Princess stands diametrically opposed to the cultural understanding between Arabs and Americans. Insecurely projected from a shadowy point of view, the docudrama solidifies stereotypes. It tells us nothing about Arab culture, let alone the execution of Princess Misha'al and her lover. Some observers of television may remember *Princess* because of the diplomatic furor. But a more important historical footnote should not be overlooked—under the guise of truth, the program exploited the Saudis, a people who are seldom given a humane image.

Documentaries

The Middle East has been the subject of documentaries on both public and commercial television as well as special news shows like CBS's *60 Minutes* and *CBS Reports,* NBC's *White Paper,* PBS's *World* and ABC's *Closeup* and *20/20.* Many of these programs, beginning with the 1975 TV season and including two 1974 documentaries, focused on the Saudis and the Palestinians. This chapter will examine how producers have depicted them. Unlike the image of Arabs in entertainment programs, an image which reinforces a negative stereotype, a number of important documentaries have offered more balanced presentations. There are almost three million Americans of Arab descent in the United States—among them an estimated 100,000 Palestinians. For the most part, entertainment television has made them out to be an "Arab peril." The documentaries we will discuss, however, evoke a variety of images, both positive and negative. Some of these documentaries, such as *The Palestinians, The Saudis, Israel and the Palestinians: Will Reason Prevail?* and *The Arabs and Israelis* have fostered a genuine understanding of these people. These evenhanded and thoughtful programs informed viewers of the importance of the Palestinians and Saudis to a peaceful Middle East settlement. The documentary producers show Arabs not as terrorists or oily sheiks but as individuals with rights and aspirations.

Like producers of television entertainment programs, documentary producers must select topics, people, camera angles, words and music appropriate to the subject. Unlike the entertainment producers, they do not invent materials. Their primary objective is to capture fragments of reality and arrange them in a meaningful manner. While the editors of the nightly news shows are always pressed for time, the documentary producer usually has more time to conduct interviews and do extensive research, write and evaluate the script and consider the overall balance of the final news package. A newscast typically lasts no more than a couple of minutes—the documentary offers twenty minutes to nearly an hour of air time on one subject. Consequently, a fairer, more complete examination of a complex subject or people is possible.

Often, however, even the most balanced programs evoke criticism from both Israeli and Arab sympathizers. Few people have any sympathy for the small minority of Palestinian or Israeli extremists. But if a documentary tries to depict Palestinians realistically, some viewers complain that the producers are pro-Palestinian. Likewise, some viewers resent documentary coverage of pro-Israeli issues. The problem of balance is perhaps best explained by Vice President of ABC News, George Watson, who said, "In our reporting of the Middle East, we frequently find that what one side praises the other condemns. Our object is to be as accurate and fair as we possibly can in our reporting."

Although producers may find it difficult to portray another culture objectively, *60 Minutes* has done a generally outstanding job on programs concerning other nations. On occasion, though, the program gives its 40 million weekly viewers unnecessary displays of staged theatrics that reduce Arabs to caricatures. While razzle-dazzle phrases and clever cinematography may entertain the viewer, the credibility of both the program and the correspondent suffers. Fairness in reporting may sometimes be less exciting to watch. But fairness is essential in television documentaries.

Two *60 Minutes* programs lacked balance. The first, "The Arabs Are Coming," with Morley Safer, aired in December 1977. In one portion, we see the correspondent sitting comfortably in the back seat of a Rolls-Royce. Next to Safer is an actor playing the part of an Arab sheik. When the Rolls-Royce stops, the "sheik" gets out. The driver asks him what to do with the car. "Keep it," he says. The program gives viewers the impression that Arabs are not only super-rich but also irresponsible. Was the Safer scene lifted from Linda Blandford's 1976 book *Oil Sheikhs*? Blandford writes in that book, "One summer in the early 1970s, a chauffeur spent two months driving a Saudi prince around in his brand new £12,000 Rolls-Royce Corniche. On the day His Highness left, the chauffeur drove him to the airport (and) asked what he was to do with the car. 'Keep it,' came the answer."

Was the title *The Arabs Are Coming* a take-off from the motion picture *The Russians Are Coming, The Russians Are Coming* (thus equating Arabs with the nation that is America's greatest threat)? Imagine the reaction had *60 Minutes* entitled a similar show "The Jews Are Coming" or "The Blacks Are Coming." Interestingly, one does not find the Safer routine with the imaginary sheik in CBS's official transcript of the program. The program implies throughout that Arabs are spending a lot of money in London. "London's been taken by storm," says Safer. The city "has experienced nothing like this invasion. They come for three or four months, and they come to buy anything that is not nailed down, plus an awful lot that is," he says. Safer, however, never interviews Arabs who are in London to study at universities, work or practice medicine, law and journalism. Instead of speaking with a cross-section of people, Safer interviews some prominent *Englishmen* who conduct business with wealthy Arabs. In these interviews, Safer offers viewers assorted "facts": 1) an English home "smells different" after an Arab has bought it; 2) Arabs have rather "garish" tastes in decorating; 3) King Khaled spent $70,000 for flowers during a three-week stay at a London hospital—"no one knows how much was spent on doctors"; 4) Arabs are "buying up bits and pieces of British history"; 5) "people may mock the Arabs behind their backs or be downright racist, but they happily accept their money."

The journalist eventually chats with a young Arab man gambling at a casino, then puzzles the viewer with this apparent contradiction: Arabs are "rarely interviewed, because it seems that (they) are a reserved, formal, stiff-upper-lip kind of people, and the volatile British do not understand them. And so it makes for some confusion." Safer's analysis concludes: "In London the cobbles echo with the cry, 'The Arabs are coming! The Arabs are coming!' "

Another *60 Minutes* segment—"The 600 Million $ Man"— contends that Arabs, especially Saudis, are buying up America. In the January 1977 program teaser, Morley Safer remarks that "Arab investment (in the U.S.) has now passed twenty billion—twenty billion dollars!—and rises about one billion a year." The report goes on to stress the importance of a Saudi Arabian named Adnan Kashoggi to Arab trade investments in the United States. Kashoggi complains that investments made by Arabs are "colored" and labeled as "Arab money" in a way that German marks and French francs are not.

Safer doesn't explain why Arab money is "colored." Nor does he mention press reports which offer evidence that the entire clamor over Arab investments in the U.S. is much overblown. Peter Arnett of the Associated Press has reported "that despite all the publicity, direct investment by Middle East powers in America remains small compared with the investment of other countries." The Los Angeles *Times* and The Washington *Post* have printed that the leading investors in American property are the Dutch, British, Canadians, Germans, Swiss, French and Japanese, in that order.

New York *Times* correspondent Seth S. King, citing Department of Agriculture figures, wrote in 1979 that "British investors own by far the largest total of agricultural land ... more than 907,000 acres," King added, "Contrary to persistent rumors that oil-rich Arabs have been pouring money into farm purchases in the South and West and inflating land prices, less than 1,500 acres is shown to be Arab-owned, according to the department."

A slightly different view of the Saudis emerges on an NBC *White Paper* entitled "No More Vietnams, But ...," which aired in September 1979, with Edwin Newman and Garrick Utley. This documentary looks at Saudi-American relations and occasionally employs visual theatrics to magnify selected scenes. The *White Paper* examines America's dependence on foreign oil as well as the civil strife in Yemen, Oman's role in guarding the strategic Strait of Hormuz, and Soviet and U.S. military power in the Middle East. During the first half of the program, which focuses on Saudi Arabia, Edwin Newman warns: "We must understand the Saudis and their problems quickly." The show gives viewers the impression that America needs the Saudis and other Arabs only because they have oil.

The report begins with stock footage showing angry and frustrated Americans waiting at the gas pumps. "Nineteen seventy-nine is the year of the gas line," says Newman. The footage and Newman's commentary suggest that because of our dependence on foreign oil—specifically Saudi oil—the Saudis are to blame if we have no gasoline.

Utley says, "the United States has been forced into a new relationship with a country and a region with which it has no cultural ties, no long-standing political partnership. A relationship which has one common denominator—oil." He neglects to point out that there were approximately 15,000 Saudi students in the United States between 1979 and 1980. Nor does he say that there are some 40,000 Americans in Saudi Arabia. Massive exchanges of people are taking place. Utley ignores the human element and dwells on the issue of oil, saying, "They have it. We need it."

The musical track which plays in the background features the song "Food for Crude." It accompanies scenes of frustrated American motorists in gas lines. We then see scenes of derricks and natural gas flames. Utley comments: "Here are the oil installations at work, built by Americans, still run largely under American supervision and which, in the case of war, would have to be defended by the United States." Is Utley suggesting that because the Saudis use our technology and employ our technicians, Saudi oil should be our oil?

Utley soon asks the viewer, "Why doesn't the United States simply help itself to some more oil? Or to put it more bluntly, why don't we take it?" Suppose a foreign country dependent on American exports decided they didn't like our prices and started talking about coming over to *take* what they want. How would we react?

Utley makes much of Saudi oil wealth, but he seldom explains what the Saudis actually do with their money. Instead, he implies only what they *could* do, saying, "The Saudis *could,* if they chose to, buy General Motors in 18 weeks, Exxon Corporation in 25 weeks, all the stocks on the New York and American stock exchanges in 18 years. Or, for something more modest, Tiffany's in 18 hours."

According to political and economic analyst John Law, "It was a popular pastime in the 1970s to figure out how many days of Arab oil production it would take to buy all of IBM (210 days). What makes this type of comparison misleading," notes Law in his book *Arab Investors,* "is the assumption that oil revenues provide the Arabs only with extra pocket money to shop around with—whereas, in fact, oil production provides virtually the entire income that the producing countries have to live on and use for their development. Using similar logic," Law says, "it could be said that the American people produce so much in goods and services each year ($2 trillion worth) that they can buy up all of Great Britain, France, West Germany, and Switzerland and still have enough money left over to buy 15 Saudi Arabias."

In short, Utley fails to note that the Saudis spend most of their money to assist the poor in Arab and other Third World nations, increase food production, acquire technological capabilities, build schools and hospitals, develop Arab natural resources, and search for alternative sources of energy. Because its small population is scattered over vast areas and its climate is temperate, Saudi Arabia is particularly suited to the application of solar power. The Solar Institute, located in Colorado, manages a $100 million solar project in Saudi Arabia—a joint venture established between the two countries in 1977. With the help of the Institute and other American companies, Saudi Arabia hopes to meet the energy needs of some villages entirely by solar power by late 1984.

Utley conducts five brief interviews with Saudi natives and concludes: "It is not easy to get to know the Saudis. Wherever you look there are homes surrounded by walls...concrete veils drawn over private life (visuals show a sequence of walls). There are other veils," says the correspondent as stills of veiled women appear. "A Saudi woman today receives an education. But there are few places where she can work." He does not mention, however, that half of all Saudi doctors are women (which was reported, interestingly enough, by Ed Bradley in the 1980 CBS documentary, *The Saudis* and by Jo Franklin-Trout in the 1983 PBS documentary, *Saudi Arabia*). The *White Paper,* instead, portrays all Saudi women as repressed. Utley neglects to probe beyond superficial images and statements.

Utley points out that Islam is the religion of the country, and quickly adds that the Royal Family "uses it" for political purposes. But he doesn't explain what he means. Do Israeli leaders "use" Judaism to justify making territorial acquisitions? Do American Senators "use" Christianity when posing for a bevy of photographers on their way to and from church on Sundays?

White Paper's producers fail to put Moslem leaders in perspective with other world leaders. For example, when Utley says "Saudi Arabia is still a nation of tribes," the producers follow his comment with a series of pictorial scenes that show the celebration of a traditional tribal ceremony. The producers do not balance this with scenes of Saudi's Royal Family discussing current problems among themselves or with their people. Nor does the correspondent show viewers Saudi lawyers, doctors or teachers.

To his credit, however, Utley carefully examines the impact of Western technology on Saudi culture. A child appears on his father's shoulder carrying a can of Pepsi. The cinematographer shows how crumbling structures are giving way to modern edifices. The viewer sees new schools and hospitals. The government spends $50 billion annually on basic development projects, Utley says.

The tidal wave of money, he notes, has brought not just instant prosperity but also traffic jams. Shots of bumper-to-bumper American cars on a Saudi street transcend cultural barriers: a traffic jam is a traffic jam. Dr. Ghazi Al-Gosaibi, Saudi Arabia's Minister of Industry, explains that his country has tried to modernize in less than a decade. Some Saudis naturally think that change is coming at an all-too-rapid pace. Some fear the loss of cherished Islamic traditions. Dr. Al-Gosaibi, for example, praises the work ethic of the West, saying that the Saudis ought to follow it in achieving their technological goals. But he tells Utley they want to avoid copying "some of the negative things of your industrial way of life...the destruction of the family...the loneliness of people." When many become old, says Al-Gosaibi, "they are thrown into an old age house."

Utley's commentary summarizes the Saudi dilemma: "The oil which has given such wealth (to the Saudis) is the oil which can destroy their traditions, and eventually the stability of their country upon which we depend so much." He speaks over a montage of the old and new—a silhouette of a mosque is intercut with neon lights and cars.

In an emergency, the Saudis must rely on American military support. The nation has become the world's largest defense spender; they have ample tanks and planes, including the American F-15s. But, as Utley points out, "Saudi Arabia does not have an army strong enough or large enough to defend itself. We are committed to defend Saudi Arabia's oil and to protect the Royal Family against domestic unrest or a military coup," he says.

For its part, the Saudis have thus far kept their distance from the Russians. Saudi Arabia has not exchanged ambassadors with the USSR or any other communist country. King Faisal was particularly outspoken in his hostility toward communism, which he maintained fostered international instability. The *White Paper*, however, fails to point out the potential influence of the Russians in the region. The correspondents say little about the possibilities of the Saudis and other Arabian Gulf nations doing business with the Soviets out of frustration with U.S. Middle East policy, or, because of the threat of Soviet force.

Another View of the Saudis

The Saudis, a CBS Special Report, was aired in October 1980. The viewing audience was not large because it appeared opposite the sixth game of the World Series—the highest-rated Series game ever. Producer Maurice Murad and correspondent Ed Bradley offered viewers a comprehensive view of Saudi society, providing the background necessary to understand the contrasts and contradictions of Saudi Arabian life. Bradley ascertained after interviewing over a dozen Saudis, from women in college to foreign ministers, that Saudi Arabia did not fit the stereotype of camel-riding tribal chieftains who practice oil blackmail. Nor is it the land of Rudolph Valentino's *The Sheik*. Rather, this documentary showed the country as a progressive, religious, yet vulnerable nation with important ties to the United States. The producers closely examine the changing nature of Saudi society, its special relationship with the United States, the vulnerability of its vast supplies of oil, and its temporal and spiritual sources of leadership—the Royal Family and the Moslem faith.

The war between Iran and Iraq which began in 1980, has caused apprehension in the West, and for good reason. The oil fields of Saudi Arabia, just 400 miles from the conflict, were practically defenseless. Bradley says that if a nation threatened Saudi oil fields, the President would probably call in American troops to defend, not take over, Saudi Arabia. "It is impossible to over-estimate Saudi Arabia's importance to the West," says Bradley. "Their 750 oil wells supply eight percent of the

U.S.'s oil, forty percent of France's, thirty-five percent of Italy's, and twenty-five percent of Japan's."

Bradley asks, "Who are the Saudis?" He explains that in 1932 Bedouin tribes became united under the House of Saud, and then outlines the development of Saudi Arabia up to the November 1979 attack by religious fundamentalists on the Holy Mosque of Mecca. As for historical monuments, Bradley says, "There is not much left of old Arabia." The Saudis now face the conflict of a society embracing modernization while retaining its orthodox ways. Indeed, the country is the world's largest construction site. The government will issue $50 billion in construction contracts in the next five years.

Bradley interviews Minister of Industry Ghazi Al-Gosaibi, who says the Saudi government "is not working against the desires of the people." He explains that Saudi leaders want the people to keep their value systems to make certain the spiritual side does not change. The minister says that Westerners are selling "the material way of life" to Saudis, and that some of these Westerners are "wheeler-dealers." But Al-Gosaibi does not blame the West entirely for his country's social and religious changes.

Bradley shows the country as a *different* society, not necessarily better or worse. He looks at the *majlis,* the Saudi version of the "town meeting." In the Kingdom's open Islamic courts, says religious scholar Mujalid Al-Sawwaf, any person—either claimant or defendant—is able to come to the court without a lawyer. Most of the people come by themselves, he says. He tells Bradley that "appeals are allowed and procedures followed." For fifteen centuries the Saudis have been ruling according to Islamic law, with the *Koran* as the chief guide. Bradley notes that the *Koran,* like the U.S. *Constitution,* adapts to changing times. The documentary respects Islam. The viewer sees Saudis praying alone, or in a crowded mosque, or in a country field by a tent. It avoids the popular, but false, stereotype of the Islamic Saudi as a religious fanatic.

One segment in the show focuses on a young government official, the American-educated Faisal Al-Bashir. This was my favorite part of the program because it reminded me of my Saudi students in the States. Al-Bashir explains to Bradley that despite his education, his tribe once considered him to be "one of the biggest failures they ever met." Al-Bashir understood their thinking: the tribe expected him to stay with them and become their leader, but he left them to pursue higher studies and civil service. Al-Bashir said that within the tribe, there is the feeling that "everyone is your cousin or a brother or a relative.... You feel together." He said that when he left his tribal community, he missed the beauty and harshness of desert life and the impact of the quiet peace that prevails there. Some producers might have measured the technological revolution in the merely material terms of traffic jams and skyscrapers rather than in human terms. Here—perhaps for the first time in a television program—a young Saudi expresses his feelings about the impact of technological progress on his family and his life.

Bradley continues to elicit Saudi self-expression. He asks women students how they feel about the law that forbids them to drive cars and about the law permitting men to have more than one wife, while they may have only one husband. Contrary to Western perceptions, though, the man with more than one wife is rare. The women he interviews wear no veils. The camera shows them playing volleyball, joking, and studying. Most of them had studied or traveled in the United States.

They said they intend to enter such fields as medicine, biology and teaching. Their teacher, a prominent Saudi educator, a woman named Cecile Rouchdy, told Bradley that their sexually-segregated society protects women and that it is unfortunate that in the West a segregated society is not acceptable. She asks, "Why should you always look upon...whatever is different from your society as wrong?"

Cecile Rouchdy's question best summarizes our current problem with some nations, including Saudi Arabia. For a Saudi, to be different means that the West fears or misunderstands him. One reason we formerly embraced the Shah of Iran was because he seemed to be Americanizing his people. The Shah was a media celebrity, a frequent guest on *60 Minutes* and network talk shows. He impressed us by his noble appearance, his Western ways, and his arms deals. Our government gave him total support. All the while, the Shah's secret police force, *Savak*, was terrorizing Iranians at home and in the United States.

Contributing editor of *Esquire* magazine, Harry Stein, has written, "Over the years...we have paid a devastating price...for our ignorance of other cultures. Our tendency—often more like a reflex—is still to support those culturally more like ourselves over those less like ourselves.... And all of us whose understanding of other cultures is constrained by ignorance...will continue to suffer a loss in our own lives."

A nation's similarity to our culture should not be the basis for approval or disapproval. The new industrial revolution shows that we can learn from others—the West Germans, Japanese—as they once learned from us. The Germans and Japanese borrowed and refined

American production methods. Now we are doing some borrowing and adapting of our own. Why can't we respect the Saudis for trying to hold onto their own identities?

At one point in *The Saudis,* U.S. Ambassador John West tells Bradley that because of unrest in the Middle East and the Palestinian problem, Saudi Arabia, traditionally a moderate OPEC member, may one day use its oil as a weapon. Saudi Arabian Foreign Minister Prince Saud Al-Faisal explains: "The Middle East is not unstable...because Saudi Arabia has large resources of oil. It is because Israel occupies Arab territories and drives the Palestinians out of their homeland." Adds Bradley: "There are over 50,000 Palestinians working in Saudi Arabia;" they are a constant reminder to the Saudis "of the unsettled issue of the Palestinian homeland."

The Saudis are now the largest purchaser of American military hardware and services in the world, Bradley says. Yet Ambassador West fears that the oil fields, containing 30 to 35 percent of the known oil resources in the world, are not easy to defend. The camera shows scenes of the Saudi army (75,000 men in the armed forces) in training. He points out that when and if the Soviets need oil, they may be able to take it—not only from Saudi Arabia, but from nearby Arab nations. "It would take at least three weeks before a major U.S. strike force could be put down on Saudi soil," Bradley says.

Several unresolved issues cloud American-Saudi relations. The Saudis are still uncertain whether the United States would defend them if there was internal strife or if the Soviets were to attack. They are confused by the U.S. position on a Palestinian homeland or state. Conversely, Americans question whether Saudi oil will continue to flow West as long as the Palestinian issue remains unsettled. Will Saudi Arabia continue to be a "moderate" in OPEC? Should American troops defend Saudi soil if the oil fields were to be attacked?

Producer Murad and correspondent Bradley provide us with a timely and sensitive analysis of Saudi Arabia. America's special relationship with Saudi Arabia "will be sorely tested in the months and years to come," concludes Bradley. As he speaks, the camera focuses on scenes of Saudi families picnicking on the beach and kids playing soccer between skyscrapers. These scenes and others humanize the Saudi people. One thing I especially liked about *The Saudis* was the music selected by the producers. They chose an old, dignified hymn. The words, though not sung on the show, explain what I believe the Saudis are trying to do:

'Tis a gift to be simple

'Tis a gift to be free
'Tis a gift to come down where we want to be...
To turn, turn, will be our delight
'Til by turning, turning, we come round right...

Palestinian Images On Public Television

The seven-part documentary series *Arabs and Israelis,* produced by WGBH in Boston in 1975, examined the prospects for peace in the Middle East. Two of the segments focused on the Palestinian question. Those interviewed spoke not of war, but of a possible peace. One Israeli said: "We didn't come here to kick them out of their country." Another pointed out that 600,000 Jews lived in Palestine by the end of the Holocaust and were safe among their Palestinian neighbors. Palestinian comments were equally expressive. One said he hoped the Israelis would recognize the PLO and the national rights of the Palestinian people. The issue at hand, he said, has been and remains "the struggle between two rights."

The PBS segments examined a variety of crucial questions. Will there be a single state or a two-state solution— Palestine and Israel? What about the fundamental matter of Jewish immigration and the return of the Palestinians? Will settlements on the West Bank continue at the expense of the Palestinians? Executive producer Peter McGhee said of the series, "We have not tried to cover all aspects of the conflict or review the history of the Middle East, to suggest who is right or wrong.... We listen instead for softer voices, those that may be easily drowned out but are no less important to hear."

McGhee worked with producer Roger Fisher, a Harvard University law professor who has said he believes "television might be an instrument for helping solve the Middle East conflict." Field producers Zvi Dor-Ner, an Israeli, and Egyptian newspaperman Mohammed Salmawy worked together closely, even though they (at the time) could not then visit each other's homelands. They said they were concerned that American viewers were being exposed only to extreme points of view and sought moderate opinions from their respective countrymen.

Watching the *Arabs and Israelis* series today remains a highly emotional experience. Grief unites, as does hope. There are no stereotypes, only individuals who possess no enmity towards each other. Those with reason to be bitter, families that have lost loved ones, speak not of violent acts of revenge but of a peaceful tomorrow. "Bound together by a mutual abhorrence of war," writes Richard Schickel in *Time* on February 17, 1975, the series "is a kind of candle sputtering bravely in the darkness."

The candle reveals a humanity that television all too often denies viewers. The series make us feel. It makes the ordinary tears of others become our own.

Another PBS documentary that investigates the current status of the Israel-Palestine conflict is John Wallach's *Israel and the Palestinians: Will Reason Prevail?*, which aired in January 1981. The absorbing program is evenly balanced with spokesmen from both sides. Wallach interviews Palestinian educators, journalists and artists as well as Israeli government leaders such as Menachem Begin, Shimon Peres, Yitzhak Rabin and General Matti Peled. The documentary also features Bethlehem's mayor Elias Freij, Yasser Arafat of the PLO, and Egypt's President Anwar el-Sadat.

In Washington, Wallach told me that presenting "a balanced documentary" was a "no-win" situation. The journalist, who works as foreign affairs editor of the Hearst Newspapers, said he had not anticipated receiving hate mail after the documentary aired. In New York, some members of the Jewish Defense League protested outside station WNET during the press review of the show. Wallach, with a modest budget of $15,000 and a staff of three, sought and obtained for viewers moderate voices. The journalist did not exploit or propagandize one point of view. "I wanted to show Palestinians not as terrorists," he said.

The producer asks tough questions of both parties. As a result of this evenhanded approach, we gain a better perspective of the Palestine-Israel question. For example, Wallach asks West Bank Palestinians and Israelis how they can achieve peace. Should there be a Palestinian state? If so, where will it be? Nearly one and a half million Palestinians live under a pervasive Israeli military occupation on the West Bank and the Gaza Strip. Many Palestinians contend that Israelis "want everybody to get out," and that the settlements will eventually bring about the annexation of the West Bank and the Gaza Strip to Israel. Wallach says that most Israelis do not want a Palestinian state. "Begin would just like the Palestinian problem to go away," he says. As for the Palestinians, they refuse to recognize a Jewish state until the Israelis first recognize a Palestinian state. A feeling of mutual distrust prevails.

The producer's unflattering portrayal of both Arafat and Begin shows them as inflexible leaders. Shimon Peres, on the other hand, recognizes that compromise is needed. "We don't want to become a dominating country." General Peled says he does not view PLO members as warmongers, but as people who desperately want peace with Israel. Mayor Freij says he wants the PLO to recognize Israel's right to exist. "There will never be a military solution to the Arab-Israeli crisis," he affirms.

Wallach shows viewers some harsh measures Israelis have taken against West Bank Palestinians. He discusses Israeli press censorship with editors of a Palestinian newspaper—Israeli censors must approve *all* copy before it's set in type. The Israeli government forbids university students to celebrate their Palestinian heritage. The president of Birzeit University, Dr. Hanna Nasir, tells Wallach the Israeli army closed the university and opened fire on students because they tried to hold a national celebration. The Israeli army also confiscated the paintings of artists from the city of Ramallah only because these artists used Palestinian flag colors in farm and prison scenes. The conflict, as *Will Reason Prevail?* presents it, is right versus right. Egypt's Sadat offers a solution: there can be no peace until Israelis and Palestinians remove prevailing attitudes of mistrust. Sadat tells Wallach that once the parties involved overcome the psychological barriers between them, peace will follow. Explains Sadat: "God told us in the *Koran* . . . if you don't have the capacity to change yourself and your attitude, nothing will be changed without you."

The documentary concludes with an appeal for a mutual recognition of rights. Wallach says Israel must "recognize that Palestinians are not simply 'terrorists', that they are doctors, lawyers and engineers who, like the scattered Jews, believe they have an historical right to a homeland." Likewise, he says, "Palestinians must recognize that Israel has a right to exist as a nation. . . . Only then, when both Israelis and Palestinians begin addressing each other's legitimate concerns will progress be made towards a settlement."

In contrast to the balanced and informative *Arabs and Israelis* series and John Wallach's *Israel and the Palestinians: Will Reason Prevail?*, PBS's documentary *West Bank Story* (which aired in March 1981), distorts reality and offers an incredible number of half-truths. PBS promoted the documentary as a balanced report about the rights of Palestinians and Israelis in the Israeli-occupied West Bank of the Jordan River, the 2,165 square miles of territory captured from Jordan in the 1967 Arab-Israeli War. *West Bank Story* begins with the narrator stating that he and the producers came to the area "to gather our own impression of what life is like for the Arabs who live here and for the Israelis who have come to settle on the West Bank." Supposedly, the documentary describes the "day-to-day reality." But it fails to focus on everyday Palestinian inhabitants. Instead, the documentary features articulate Americans of Jewish faith who have recently found a home in Israel. The film portrays them as constantly threatened by the

Palestinians. Conversely, the producers neither show nor discuss Israeli acts of violence against Palestinians on the West Bank.

Several scenes show Israeli men and women carrying guns as they go to pray or shop at an Arab *souq*. They fear an attack by Palestinians who carry no arms but resent Israelis living on their land. The narrator does not tell us that Palestinians may need protection from those Israelis who have taken away their rights, confiscated their lands, and control their cities. His constant caustic observations demean those few Palestinians that appear. In one scene, for example, we begin to empathize with small Palestinian school children. The narrator then interjects: "Several students told us that they admired Ayatollah Khomeini. They have pictures of him, but asked us not to film them." The reference to Khomeini causes our perceptions of the children to change. How can we like kids who admire the Ayatollah?

By contrast, the camera shows us lovable Israeli children. The viewer never sees any educated Palestinian families, although the number of Palestinians holding university degrees is exceptionally high. "Their industry and zeal for learning (20 out of every 1,000 are in a college or university somewhere) have earned them the sobriquet 'the Jews of the Arab world'," reports *Time*. What we do see are scattered glimpses of some poor and bitter Palestinian farmers with vegetable gardens and goats. One reason they are bitter is because the Israelis limit their water, and thus their once fertile fields are now barren. Nearby we see Israeli "settlers" with guns. They want, and eventually obtain, the farmer's land. Yet the juxtaposition of shots plus the narrator's edged tone suggest that Israelis will better utilize Palestinian land. One might expect sympathy for those forced off their land. In this case, however, the producers make us sympathize with those taking the land.

On the West Bank, "thousands of acres have been expropriated from—or prohibited from use by—Palestinian Arabs," writes *Reader's Digest* reporter Edward Hughes (in the May 1980 issue). Hughes reports that "Israeli civilians continue to settle in the occupied territory, often taking over land tilled or possessed by Arabs for generations." Says Hughes, "Near Bethlehem, at least 22 Arab farmers from the village of El Hadr now have to find odd jobs to feed their families. Some 500 acres of land they have cultivated for generations have been expropriated for. . .an Israeli settlement."

Hughes writes that "other Arab farms were virtually destroyed (in the summer of 1979) because Israeli occupation officials refused to let the farmers in Al Auja drill a village well into the big underground water supplies below." Adds Hughes, "These are tapped for the exclusive use of nearby Israeli settlements, where swimming pools are brimming and well-watered grapevines and citrus trees make a fine splash of green on the scorched limestone foothills."

Israeli troops took away most of Arab bus driver Mohammed Ibrahim Issa's one-acre site, notes Hughes. The troops "unrolled barbed wire around three-fourths of his property. Down went his fig trees, lemon trees and grapevines, and onto the plot went a dozen little pre-fab homes. His frantic pleas to the local Israeli military governor were ignored.... Now Mohammed is left with just enough room for his house, a place to park his bus, and a tiny plot beside the house to grow vegetables."

The number of Jewish settlements and population on the West Bank increases each year. *U.S. News and World Report* reported that the "latest official" figures are 107 settlements with a population of about 25,000 people. The Associated Press reported in 1980 that Rabbi Emmanuel Jakobvits, chief rabbi of Great Britain, called for the establishment of a Palestinian state. Rabbi Jakobvits also publicly urged moderate Israelis, Arabs and Westerners to help in its creation, in order to avoid a new Middle East war. Rabbi Jakobvits condemned Israel's settlement policy saying, "There is nothing in the Torah that justifies the building of settlements in the land of others...." The Torah, said the rabbi, "does not call on Israelis to hold Palestinians captive in an occupation they imposed on them, and the Torah does not tell us to deprive the Palestinians of their lawful right to self-determination." He added: "I am for the establishment of a Palestinian state. I am convinced there shall be no real peace unless we are able to reach the right solution for the Palestinians."

As more Israelis establish homes in these settlements, it becomes increasingly difficult to believe that Israel would ever relinquish the West Bank. Producers of *West Bank Story* not only ignore the pervasiveness of settlements, but they omit complaints against Israeli policy that flow in from the United Nations—including the United States.

In *Reader's Digest*, reporter Hughes tells of "fifty-nine prominent American Jews," including Jerome B. Weisner, president of the Massachusetts Institute of Technology, and composer-conductor Leonard Bernstein, who published an open letter stating that "a policy which requires expropriation of Arab land unrelated to Israel's security needs and which presumes to occupy permanently a region populated by 750,000 Palestinian Arabs, we find morally unacceptable...."

West Bank Story also neglects those Israelis advocating peace and opts to feature instead on the hardliners. Reporter Hughes notes that: "A vocal and articulate minority of Israelis...support the budding Peace Now movement which took root in 1978 when both the government and opposition parties seemed reluctant to follow up Sadat's peace overture." One Peace Now founder, Omri Padan, told Hughes, "We were ready to give up territory on all fronts, including the West Bank, in exchange for a guarantee of our security." The reporter points out that, "On the eve of the Camp David talks in 1978, Peace Now organized a demonstration in Tel Aviv that brought out 100,000 Israelis to cheer them on—the biggest demonstration in Israel's history."

The producers of *West Bank Story*, however, imply that Israelis are victims of the present conflict and that the Palestinians are the victimizers. This superficial perspective of the Palestine-Israel issue shows us neither tears as in *Arabs and Israelis*, nor balanced interviews as in *Will Reason Prevail?* Instead, the PBS documentary emphasizes ordinary prejudices, complete with glaring omissions and slanted editing.

Palestinian Images On Commercial Television

An April 1980 national poll showed that thirty percent of the U.S. public think of the Palestinians as terrorists. This view has been widespread for quite a while and was the subject of a 1974 segment of *60 Minutes.* In this program, correspondent Mike Wallace shows viewers a Palestinian mother flaunting a gun, saying, "The gun will always be with us, always, always." The camera then shows the tragic results of Palestinian raids on Maalot and Kiryat Shemona. Viewers empathize, as they should, with Israeli victims. However, the documentary only briefly mentions the Israeli raids on Beirut, Lebanon. Viewers are unable to empathize with Lebanese or Palestinian casualties.

The *60 Minutes* segment suggests that all Palestinians are born radical and remain so. It ignores Israeli terror tactics and also the plight of four and a half million Palestinian refugees scattered throughout the world.

Another *60 Minutes* program, "...By What It Will Do to the Arabs," however, does point up Israeli aggression against Arabs in Israel. In this February, 1981 broadcast, correspondent Mike Wallace documents how Israel has expropriated Arab land. We see Israelis refuse a Bedouin both land and water for his flock. The correspondent explains that "special funds" for Israeli settlements finance a water line—but only Israelis may use the water.

A Palestinian professor at the University of Haifa tells Wallace: "The whole issue between Palestinians and Jewish-Zionists is land." He explains that "when Jews are brought here they need land." Most Arabs must sell or they will be forced off their land. This is nothing new. Since 1948 Israelis have expropriated thousands of acres of Arab land.

The correspondent asks an Israeli official: "How much of a threat to Israel's security are the Arabs of Israel?" "For about 32 years we had practically not even one case when an Israeli Arab fired at an Israeli policeman or soldier," says the official. Surprisingly, since 1948, out of approximately 450,000 Israeli Arabs, only about 400 have joined "terrorist groups," he says.

The documentary shows that Israelis perceive resident Palestinians as intruders. Wallace meets with several Israelis who say: "I don't particularly want to live with them." "It can't be that bad for them." "Why haven't they fled in 32 years?" "Generally, Arabs hate us Jews." "They deserve to be second-class citizens." Wallace then points to his Arab interpreter, Najji, who had studied at San Diego State, and asks: "Does he deserve to be second class?" They reply, "No."

This segment of *60 Minutes* also reveals that very little interaction occurs among Arabs and Jews. A woman who had lived in Israel for thirteen years, for example, had never met an Arab, until Najji. Najji explains to the correspondent that he has "nothing against Jews," but he is opposed to Zionism. He says that he wants harmony, not war: "I think the Jews themselves can change the Zionist aspect of the state—it can be more democratic for Arabs...just don't oppress me." Concludes Wallace: "There are some who say, 'Israel the oppressed became the oppressor'."

One of the most sensitive and balanced portrayals of the Palestinian plight was Howard Stringer's 1974 documentary for CBS, *The Palestinians*. Stringer's program won the Overseas Press Club award for the best documentary on foreign affairs in 1977. The thesis of the documentary is that "there can be no peace in the Middle East before there is peace between the Palestinians and the Israelis." The initial scenes show Palestinians firing at one another at a training camp. "That's live ammunition they're firing," says narrator Bill McLaughlin. He then explains that the "extreme fringe" of the Palestinians caused the massacre at Maalot.

The producers show us Palestinian guerrillas in Lebanon under fire as well as enjoying traditional songs. McLaughlin comments: "They are fighting for an impossible cause, a socialist Palestine made up of Arabs and Jews." In the Middle East, the "promised land," which

Israel now occupies, has been promised to two different people at the same time. The Arabs say that history confirms it belongs to the Palestinians, McLaughlin explains, while the Israelis believe God promised Israel to them.

A montage showing the history of Palestine appears. McLaughlin tells the beginning of the conflict, citing the 1917 Balfour Declaration. We then see the persecuted, homeless Jews of Nazi Germany. Scenes of the early Palestinian refugee camps resulting from the 1948 and 1967 wars are also shown. A Palestinian mother comforts her frightened child while McLaughlin explains that the Palestinians, "ignored by the West and used by the East," have been the consistent losers in the four wars fought in their name during this century. As the montage concludes, one has sympathy for both Palestinian and Jew.

In Lebanon, McLaughlin visits one of the many refugee camps and speaks with members of the Yamani family. Maher tells McLaughlin that he believes it is wrong to kill Israeli civilians, Maher says that he and most Palestinian guerrillas are concerned with attacking only military targets. Maher's parents promise that Palestinians will continue to fight. Waving a pistol, Mr. Yamani exclaims that, "We Palestinians cannot accept a piece of our land as charity from another country."

McLaughlin interviews other Palestinians, including members of the middle-class. In Beirut, he talks with a civil engineer who says he would willingly give up his wealth to live in Palestine. He says he wants to live and develop land there as he has done in other Arab countries.

McLaughlin also speaks with the Costandis, a middle-class Palestinian family in Lebanon. These educated, peace-loving people tell him that the world ignored the Palestinian refugees for nearly twenty-five years. Violet Costandi says that she and others can live with the Jews, as they once did in Palestine. To her, Palestine is home: "I was born there; I belong there."

McLaughlin also meets with Elias Freij, mayor of occupied Bethlehem. Freij advocates an independent Palestinian state on the West Bank, saying, "I announce that we accept and recognize the existence of Israel. But I ask Israel to accept our existence here." He questions Freij as to whether a Palestinian state on the West Bank would actually bring peace. Perhaps some Palestinians would not be satisifed and would want "to destroy Israel," he says. Replies Freij, "If you find a Palestinian who says he wants to destroy Israel, he's a foolish man. Israel is a fact. Israel is here to stay." McLaughlin asks, "What's the Israeli occupation like?" (At the time of the telecast in 1974, there were only 17 Israeli settlements on the West Bank). "It is an occupation," he concludes, "like any occupation."

Scenes at a training camp in Lebanon show Palestinians completing a six-month basic training course. McLaughlin says that while they appear on the surface to be a formidable force, they have no planes and no artillery. "If the guerrillas had a home," he says, "there would be no reason to fight."

McLaughlin interviews Yasser Arafat, who says that if the Israelis withdrew from the West Bank, he would establish a Palestinian state. "We want to live with the Jews," he says.

The conclusion of Stringer's documentary presents Palestinian guerrillas at leisure as they dance to an Arab folk song. They are, for the moment, at peace. The camera pulls back to show the beauty of Lebanon's countryside. Says McLaughlin: "Their promised land has yet to be delivered."

When I interviewed producer Howard Stringer, he told me, "I think where television has failed is that it doesn't do a great deal of current affairs programming. It hasn't done enough of in-depth news documentaries to correct stereotypes; hour-long documentaries should be stepping into the breach." Explained Stringer, "Before I made the film about the Palestinians, people said I was going to perpetuate the stereotype. I think we've misunderstood the Arab world pretty consistently. Members of the Lebanese government couldn't believe the film was actually shown on network television. They didn't anticipate a program that would give credence to some of the Palestinian aspirations." Stringer told me that he had no trouble from the network in the conception or production of the film. Bill Leonard, Vice President of CBS News at the time, approached Stringer about making a documentary on the Arab world. "It was my idea to do something on the Palestinians," said Stringer. "Believe me, I never had any pressure on that broadcast."

"I worked very hard to show that Arabs were not all sheiks," Stringer said. "There are middle-class and wealthy Palestinians." The documentary focuses on both Israeli and Palestinian points of view. Producer Stringer does not propose any simple solution and does not invent a villain. The documentary, however, does help explain precisely why the prospects for a peaceful settlement seem so remote and why the Palestinian problem is unlikely to disappear.

His documentary was unusual for 1974 because it suggested that a rationale existed for the idea of a West Bank Arab state. The film features an Arab saying he would live on a rooftop in Jericho if it meant the formation of a Palestinian state on the West Bank. Stringer's film concludes that the Israelis on the West Bank, whether they like it or not, have the role of an army of occupation, a role that breeds resentment and will one day have to be resolved.

Another major television documentary about Palestinians was ABC's *Terror in the Promised Land,* broadcast in October 1978. Producer Malcolm Clarke, an Englishman like Stringer, produced, wrote and directed the documentary. Clarke gives a rare sympathetic view of Palestinian guerrillas and attempts to explain what motivates them to sacrifice their lives for a land from which their friends and families were driven.

We see the film through the eyes of young Palestinians—the youngest is sixteen—who volunteer for suicide squads. They express their mission:

We go on suicidal missions because we have a cause and a principle and a land.
Better to die in one's own land than outside of it.
We are happy because I know if I go, there will be others to follow.

The ABC production unit spent weeks in the Middle East seeking out these men, trying to understand why they had chosen to sacrifice their lives. The documentary begins with three young Palestinians appearing in a "home movie." The men appear innocent of instigating terror. While they smile, the camera cuts to an explosion of a building. Inside, the same three youths, along with their Israeli captives, are blown to pieces.

Viewers see a "martyrs' cemetery" in Beirut. Photographs are neatly placed above the graves of those men who sacrificed themselves for "the cause." Narrator Frank Reynolds explains: "The men knew they were going to die, and also knew they would never be forgotten." We see some more shots of the suicide squad. When their mission ends, they, too, may enter the same cemetery.

The program includes a penetrating interview with a Lebanese businessman who supports the Palestinian cause and asks why it is so hard for the West to understand the Palestinian need to regain his identity in his own land. The businessman, Mustafa Zein, says that anyone of the Jewish faith coming from Russia or the United States "automatically has the right to settle in Israel and to have a passport." He wants to know "why people expect the Palestinians to be less patriotic than the Israelis." Following his comments, viewers witness film footage of Hitler's Holocaust. Reynolds then documents the terror—Jewish and Arab—that took place in Palestine prior to and during 1948. We see the destruction of the King David Hotel in 1947, but Reynolds does not mention that Prime Minister Menachem Begin was then a leader of Irgun, the Jewish terrorist group responsible for the hotel explosion and deaths.

Reynolds says, "There is no dispute. Palestinians had lived here for centuries in the land which is now the state of Israel." The editor juxtaposes scenes of Palestinians beginning their exile in 1948 with shots of today's refugee camps. A shot of a tranquil Arab farmer, alone with his flock, suggests peace is possible.

Another compelling segment in *Terror* features Anna Kanafani, the widow of Palestinian intellectual Ghassan Kanafani, who describes the assassination of her husband. Mrs. Kanafani, who teaches now in a refugee camp, says that Israelis assassinated other Palestinian civilians besides her husband. Narrator Reynolds then lists Palestinian officials killed by Israeli raids or by Israeli agents since Kanafani's assassination. The photographs of ten Palestinian leaders appear on the screen, framed in dark colors.

Terror shows us children making toy grenades in school. These children are taught by their elders to dance and sing about a land they have never seen. The camera cuts from a school to barbed wire, showing the innocence of childhood transformed into the reality of warfare. An eleven-year-old receives rigorous training in a refugee camp. One day he may be a guerrilla—perhaps a member of a suicide squad.

The documentary also gives credence to the accusation that Israel has tortured Palestinians. A young Palestinian student, Khalid Rubo, describes how he was severely beaten by Israelis. As he speaks, photographs of his badly bruised body appear. An American Red Cross official confirms the torture of some Palestinians in Israeli prisons. The official shared his concern with the U.S. Department of State. But, "to do that without authorization was contrary to Red Cross policy," states Reynolds, "and the Red Cross official was dismissed" from his position.

Terror concludes as it began, with the death of a young Palestinian. As narrator Reynolds says, he is "a victim as well as a perpetrator of terror in the promised land, the land of Moses, Mohammed and Jesus."

Most television critics agreed that *Terror* was an example of good broadcast journalism. In a 1979 *New Yorker* magazine article, Michael Arlen wrote: "The ABC documentary showed us more about the Palestinians in fifty-seven minutes than most American news organizations, large or small, have printed or televised in the past dozen years—and showed it with an uncommon mixture of judgment and perspective." Arlen said that the program "went after a difficult and controversial subject and communicated it with clarity and a respect for history as well as for human feelings."

As Arlen noted, the documentary was not commercially sponsored. Instead, the network aired public service announcements for the United Way, the American Lung Association, the National Cancer Institute, the Soil Conservation Service, the International Association of Police, and the Department of Health, Education and Welfare. ABC had to remove all paid commercials, according to a network spokeswoman, because it failed to give the usual six sponsors sufficient notice on the controversial nature of the program.

United Press International reported that the program attracted three thousand protest calls to ABC stations around the country, and that half the calls came in *before* the program aired. An ABC spokeswoman said many of the callers read prepared statements. She also said that some people apparently *pressured* others to call in and complain.

In New York, Clarke told me he had received no interference from the network in making or airing his work, but that the film had to be locked in a safe every night. "We took the film off the benches and out of the cans, off the machines and locked it up," he said. Because of death threats made against his life and lives of others at ABC, the network paid a private security agency to open mail addressed to members of the production team.

Clarke said, "The *Closeup* documentary unit at ABC was very brave to put *Terror* on because there was a lot of pressure." He expressed the highest regard for his executive producer, Pamela Hill, because she was so courageous "in fighting some of the hysterical opposition that came from the outside."

I asked Clarke what he had accomplished with *Terror*. He replied: "I'm proud it got on the air. I'm proud because the film showed the human face of the Palestinians fighting a cause they believe in. It addressed issues that were fresh and it addressed them honestly." Clarke explained that "in the past, with some notable exceptions, the Palestinians have not been unmasked. Up till now, no one has confronted the reality that, face to face, the 'terrorist' is a sixteen-year-old kid from a refugee camp." After a long pause, he told me, "That's frightening—when you realize that the kid is only sixteen and that he may never be seventeen."

After a network airs a documentary, it usually makes the film available to groups for a nominal rental fee. University professors, such as myself, regularly receive network documentaries for use in film courses. CBS and ABC, however, refuse to rent two documentaries that show balanced views of Palestinians. Howard Stringer's *The Palestinians*, wrote CBS's Dolores Shea, is available "on a purchase basis only, at the cost of $600." Malcolm Clarke's *Terror* is not available—for purchase or rental. According to ABC's Celeste Chin: "Please be advised that due to *legal restrictions* (emphasis added), the above program *(Terror)* is not available for distribution of any kind domestically for non-television use." Ms. Chin did not specify those "legal restrictions" preventing *Terror* from being distributed.

While ABC's *Terror* humanized the Palestinians, the network's *20/20* series perpetuated the theme that all Palestinians are terrorists who enjoy killing others, in an April 1981 segment called "The Unholy War."

Consider the opening of the program in which host Hugh Downs says, "Geraldo Rivera goes behind the lines with PLO terrorists" and "the PLO has made the world its battleground." "War" continually calls Palestinians terrorists. There are over fifty references to terror, terrorism and terrorist in all. Downs, on the other hand, praised the "elite Israeli forces stalking the enemy throughout the world," saying they are the "world's toughest intelligence forces." Robert Pierpoint of CBS News has stated that when it comes to the Middle East crisis, "the United States seems to have lost its sense of fair play and justice, and seems to be operating on a double standard." Explains Pierpoint: "For so long, Americans have become used to thinking of the Israelis as the good guys and the Arabs as the bad guys, that many react emotionally along the lines of previous prejudices. Both sides have killed innocents," notes the correspondent. "Both sides have legitimate grievances and the illegitimate methods of expressing them." Says Pierpoint, we need "a more studied balance and fair play to the difficult problems of the Middle East."

The early seconds of "War" define the program's thrust—it's the Israeli cowboys against the Palestinian Indians. We know who the winner will be, but how will the story develop? Will there be sufficient violence to sustain viewer interest? What about the massacres and battles? Have no fear, "War" is action-packed. Downs, for example, compares the Israelis to the world's best-known super-sleuth. "Remember James Bond, the fictional special agent certified to kill? Well, Israel has dozens of James Bonds," says Downs, "maybe hundreds. Young, tough, smart. They travel the world and they kill."

Killing is what "War" is all about. There are sweeping apocalyptic images and statements about Palestinian terror. Stock footage and selected interviews with radical-types document only acts of terror committed by Palestinians. In an attempt to prove that the name Palestinian means the same as terrorist, Rivera meets with several prisoners in Israeli jails who tell him they are willing to kill anyone who tries to take their land. Rivera omits moderate voices. Instead, he features the voices of bitter, imprisoned men. Their violent statements mislead viewers into thinking that those men reflect the hearts and minds of the Palestinian people.

Rivera interviews an Israeli who describes in horrifying detail how a Palestinian brutally murdered an Israeli girl while her father watched. In contrast to the Palestinians, whom we perceive through a glass darkly, we never see the Israelis sinking to the level of their enemy. An Israeli officer tells Rivera he doesn't want to kill, as it causes you to "lose something of your soul." An Israeli general who assassinated several Palestinians in Lebanon softly says, "Our soldiers are not killers."

Rivera is not the only correspondent on the scene. ABC's "hidden camera" also acts as a roving reporter. After a few shots of an Israeli prison, Rivera asserts that prison conditions for Palestinians are "adequate." There exists no deeper probing for information beyond this glimpse. Yet torture of Palestinian prisoners is a well-documented fact. *Washington Post* correspondents T.R. Reid and Edward Cody in their story, "U.S. Reports Indicate Israeli Abuse of Palestinians" in February 1979, cite a confidential State Department memo which stated: "Physical mistreatment is systematically used on many Arab security suspects interrogated in the West Bank."

Israeli lawyer Felicia Langer writes, "The use of torture during (Israeli) investigations is a method, and I declare it as a lawyer who has dealt with thousands of cases. I have seen marks of torture on the bodies of hundreds of my (Palestinian) clients. I knew prisoners who grew mad as a result of torture (or who were) half-paralyzed after a 'treatment' by electric shocks.... Many people have died in prison as a result of torture, or condemned to a slow death because of a lack of medical treatment."

The London *Times* published in 1979 the results of a five-month independent study by an "insight team" into Israel's use of torture against Palestinian detainees and prisoners. In part, its findings reveal that "torture of Arab prisoners is so widespread and systematic that it cannot be dismissed as 'rogue cops' exceeding orders. It appears to be sanctioned as deliberate policy."

"War" is a disturbing work. *20/20* is not staffed by incompetent men and women, but by professionals with varied experiences in news-gathering and reporting. ABC had no excuse for airing "War" as a documentary. How can a knowledgeable staff of correspondents and producers imply that Palestinians relish killing, while Israelis kill with regret and only out of self-defense? How can we accept the implication that the life of one person is worth more than the life of another?

"It is undeniable that, in covering the conflict between Palestinians and Israelis," writes *TV Guide* reporter John Weisman, "the U.S. networks are much more likely to give the Israeli perspective than they are to voice Palestinian concerns." Weisman reports that *"TV Guide* reviewed 10 months of coverage on the nightly news shows from logs and tapes supplied by Vanderbilt University Television News Archives—from July 1980 through April 1982. There were 38 reports of raids and retaliations by both sides; 24 of the 38 were Israeli raids on Palestinian targets in south Lebanon. Only three of these reports—for a total of one minute, ten seconds—showed pictures of the effects of the Israeli attacks. None showed any Palestinian victims. On the other hand," says Weisman, "of the 14 reports of Palestinian raids and attacks on Israel during the period, 11 included pictures of Israeli victims, and the filmed reports totaled some 17 minutes."

Since the early 70s, the Israeli Air Force and Army, using American planes and weapons, have killed thousands of Lebanese and Palestinian men, women and children. Moreover, thousands are now homeless as a result of these acts of aggression. These incursions into Lebanon at times involved documented illegal use of American-supplied weapons. Both broadcast and print journalists have reported these invasions, massive strafings and bombings, and have photographed scenes of the dead and the suffering. "War" omits Israeli acts of aggression. By providing viewers with religious misinformation, "War" fails also to grasp the realities of the Lebanese conflict. Rivera says the Christian Lebanese and the Moslem Palestinians are fighting each other. Thus, viewers are led to assume all Lebanese are Christians and all Palestinians are Moslem. In fact, there are both Palestinian and Lebanese Christians and Moslems. The war in Lebanon has more to do with Lebanese class conflicts than with religion.

The late Lebanese Christian leader Bashir Gemayel appears in "War" as a champion of freedom against the Palestinian Moslems. Rivera shows Gemayel mourning the loss of his young daughter. The scene suggests she is "the victim of (Palestinian) terror." But Rivera fails to say that her death was the result of Lebanese inter-Christian rivalry. Gemayel had previously ordered the execution of the son of the former President of Lebanon, Suleiman Franjeeh, a fellow Lebanese-Christian. Franjeeh's son Tony, his wife, his 18-month-old daughter, and thirty of his followers were brutally executed.

I was teaching communications at the American University of Beirut in 1974-75, when the civil strife began. The war is complex and demonstrates that no simple solution exists. Outside intervention from East and West plays an important role. Russian and American-made weapons as well as arms from other nations help perpetuate the senseless killings that still take place in war-ravaged Lebanon. Everyone, and no one, shares the blame for this tragedy.

A few months after "War," ABC's *20/20* again enhanced the stereotype of Palestinians as throngs of terrorists in a program entitled "If You Were President"—a staged study of how America's leaders would operate during a terrorist attack. The show appeared in August, 1981. "President" is clearly a work of fiction, but it was telecast as a special one-hour *news* program. In "President," several government officials, were chosen for their roles by *20/20* "for their experience with past crises," explains host Downs.

The plot reveals Palestinians threatening to blow up an oil tanker, located near the World Trade Center, unless the United States supports the establishment of a Palestinian state on the West Bank. Seymour Weiss, former director of the State Department's Bureau of Political and Military Affairs, takes the role of White House chief of staff. When he hears the Palestinian request for statehood plus $1 billion, Weiss says, "There is no way the President can accept these kinds of demands. They're obviously outrageous."

During this fictional drama, we also learn that if the "terrorists" explode the tanker, the lives of "several million people" would be involved. As with ABC's "The Unholy War," the producers of "President" make over fifty references to terrorist, terrorism and terror.

Israeli journalist Uri Avneri writes, Some "PLO were called 'terrorists,' but then it started being applied to all PLO members, be they diplomats, officials, physicians, nurses." Avneri explains, "When a journalist lends a hand to the dehumanization of an entire people, then the blood of those people can be spilt freely. We, the Jews, know this better than anyone else. Once a Jew is described as subhuman, he can be killed with impunity. Once a Palestinian refugee is described as a 'terrorist,' he can be bombed, shelled, expelled and denied human rights and dignity."

As fiction, "President" should not have appeared in *20/20*—a major network *news* series. The producers do not mention that there are terrorist groups in Puerto Rico, Germany, Italy, England, Ireland, Israel and Japan. Why were the Palestinians singled out? Why didn't the producers and/or ex-government officials involved insist that the villains in "President" remain anonymous as an ethnic group?

Yet *20/20* did offer a more humane and insightful approach to the Palestinians' plight with its February, 1982, segment called "Under the Israeli Thumb." This program examined what life is like for Palestinians living under Israeli occupation.

"This is my property, my life. I have titles to prove this land is mine," says one impoverished Palestinian farmer to ABC correspondent Tom Jarriel. But the farmer's land will be bulldozed to make way for a new Israeli settlement. Such settlements are what the U.S. government calls "obstacles to peace." Jarriel explains that "under Israeli military occupation, the Arab farmer will lose [his land]. The Israeli settler is backed up by the army."

Palestinian economist Ibrahim Mattar tells Jarriel, "We are witnessing the final phases of the liquidation of Palestine. And it is being done now, acre after acre." The camera reveals an elderly farmer cutting his orchard into firewood. Although Israelis deny farmers water for crops, a nearby Israeli settlement has plenty of water for irrigation— and a new swimming pool.

We witness Palestinian school girls from Ramallah being shot and wounded by Israeli soldiers. Also, two West Bank mayors appear— whose legs have been blown off, allegedly by ultra-conservative Israelis. At a hospital, Jarriel explains that "the infant mortality rate is going up." A Palestinian doctor says: "Babies who need respirators, and don't get them, die." Israelis admit there is only "one baby respirator at the Ramallah hospital." But at an "Israeli hospital serving the same size population," reports Jarriel, "there are ten baby respirators."

20/20's executive producer, Av Westin, has said that ABC tried to include Israeli officials in the program. But the officials—including defense minister Ariel Sharon—refused. Westin contends that "Thumb" was not "one of those balanced pieces in which both sides get equal time. But in the continuing coverage by the ABC News Division," added Westin, "I would say that the Israelis get the preponderance of the coverage."

In September, 1982, about a thousand Palestinian refugees, children, women and the elderly, were massacred at Beirut's Sabra and Shatila camps. In the aftermath of this tragedy, ABC produced a memorable program, "Oh, Tell the World What Happened . . . ." This documentary examines how the Palestinians were murdered, why the slaughter took place and who was responsible for the carnage. ABC News correspondent Bill Redeker interviews dozens of eyewitnesses

Palestinian survivors, Lebanese militiamen and officials, and Israeli journalists, politicians and military officers.

Redeker asks: "How could a massacre happen on Israeli-occupied territory, controlled by Israeli forces?" The correspondent then explains that "the Phalange soldiers (Christian militiamen) ... are directly responsible. But their deeds were made possible by the negligence of others." The correspondent explains that Israeli officers permitted the Phalange to enter the camps. And that the United States and Lebanese governments share the blame because they failed to protect the Palestinians.

In "Oh, Tell The World What Happened ..." we witness scores of bullet-ridden bodies; whole families, half-buried in debris. Mauled corpses—a back, a head, a leg—are bulldozed into massive graves.

The documentary's most telling moments take place when survivors of the massacre speak: "My sisters and brothers are all gone. I am the only one left. We were about twenty-five people—boys, girls and women. And we hadn't hurt anyone. So why did they come and kill us?"

"We are still afraid," says another survivor. "And we will be afraid. Where will we go? Who will take care of us?"

The program concludes with correspondent Redeker saying: "When the names of Sabra and Shatila have faded, there will still be questions. Questions about the motives of men too long at war."

Once again the regular commercial sponsors of an ABC documentary series withdrew their commercial messages from a program. ABC's Sharon R. Rehme, manager, product acquisition/distribution, told me, " 'Oh, Tell the World What Happened....' is not available for videocassette distribution." The documentary cannot be rented or purchased. ABC's 'Under the Israeli Thumb', said Rehme, is available for distribution...on a purchase only basis, $305.

The father of the documentary, John Grierson, has said that the documentarist's best work is accomplished, "not by searchlight but in the quiet light of ordinary humanism." Documentarists seek to convey such humanism by making controversial and complex issues more easily understood.

But documentarists sometimes generate misconceptions.

A case in point is the *CBS Reports* program entitled "Death of a King: What Changes for the Arab World?" which aired in March, after King Faisal of Saudi Arabia was assassinated. Saudi Arabia is the world's largest oil producer with the greatest proven reserves. The King's death naturally caused some anxiety, raising questions about who would become his successor and whether the new ruler would continue to follow Faisal's pro-Western stance.

To answer some of these questions and others, CBS News presented "Death of a King" with correspondents Charles Collingwood, Bill McLaughlin and Marvin Kalb approximately twelve hours after Faisal's death. Technically, it was a worthy achievement. The producers edited and mixed stock footage with scenes from current happenings in the Kingdom. McLaughlin analyzed the impact of the assassination on Arab and Western countries. The film, however, contained a number of innuendoes and speculations that left viewers with wisps of exotic mysteries instead of documented facts.

Correspondent Kalb told Collingwood that the assassination wasn't really much of a surprise. Said Kalb: "Every time we would go into Riyadh with Kissinger (Kalb had recently been in Saudi Arabia with Henry Kissinger), you would have the feeling that ... it was an environment for plotters." Added Kalb: "People were walking around and there was the constant shifting of eyes."

The "shifty-eyed" and "environment for plotters" statements went unchallenged by Collingwood. In a personal note to a friend, Collingwood defended Kalb but admitted the special "contained errors of fact and of interpretation." He explained that "this is too often the case in the handling of quick-breaking events."

As Mark Twain wrote, "The difference between the right word and the almost right word is the difference between lightning and the lightning bug." Political analyses based on evidence such as "shifty eyes" cannot be tolerated. Remember, the shameful internment of Japanese-Americans during World War II was based, to some extent, on their having "funny" eyes.

This CBS news report and the documentaries examined illustrate that ignorance breeds stereotypes and suggest that peace and security will come only when mutual respect and trust occur between Israelis and Palestinians.

Film-maker Jacob Bender, an American Jew, and Kamal Boullata, a Palestinian artist, are working together to produce a documentary, *Abraham's Children*. The film will focus on the oral histories of three Palestinians and three Israelis. The message of *Abraham's Children*, says Bender, is that the path to peace must begin with a dialogue between Palestinians and Israelis. Such a dialogue can lead to mutual understanding and compromise between both peoples.

George Watson, vice president of ABC News, has said: "Generally, Arabs have not been seen to be as real, as close, or as tangible either as individuals or as a group, as the Israelis. We have been very close to them

(Israelis) and we have not been that close to the Arab world," said Watson. "Is that a failing on the part of the media? To a degree, perhaps, because we certainly would hope that part of our role is opening our eyes and vistas to subjects and problems that people might not otherwise be aware of," Watson said.

More objective documentaries are essential if we are to better understand the problems and the peoples of the Middle East. As producer Howard Stringer said, "Hour-long documentaries should be stepping into the breach. "Television," said Stringer, "has not done enough in-depth documentaries to correct stereotypes." Let us hope that *Abraham's Children* and other documentaries will open "our eyes and vistas" and offer viewers fair perspectives. Unlike the entertainment program, the main objective of the television documentary is to inform and to enlighten—to provide viewers with facts, questions and points of view that make us a more knowledgeable people.

Overview

As of this writing the future of the TV Arab is unclear. The stereotype remains omnipresent, appearing in new programs and dated reruns. As writer Irving Pearlberg (*Police Woman*) told me: "What you get on TV today is old stereotypes of older shows and movies, plus new stereotypes of current shows and movies." Those writers and producers who view the Arab world and its people in a characteristic way transfer their beliefs, consciously or unconsciously, from old to new productions. It is a serious matter, considering that these entertainment programs not only reach ninety million viewers nightly throughout the United States, but an additional four billion people watch American TV shows "in 133 international markets," according to media trade journals.

What can television professionals do to change all this? I believe that writers, producers and broadcast standards executives must first recognize the stereotyping problem and then make a commitment to do something about it.

Some people in the profession were not even aware of the ways in which the Arabs are stereotyped. Frank Glicksman, for example, the executive producer of the *Trapper John, M.D.* series asked me: "Is there enough material to support a book?" I was not surprised at Glicksman's question. Several of his associates had previously expressed similar doubts about whether a TV Arab image even exists.

Broadcast Standards and Practices divisions of all major networks also seemed unaware of the plethora of the negative images on television until my initial letters of concern in the 1970s. Since then they have welcomed an exchange of information and ideas. Early reaction was mixed. NBC's Jerome Stanley said: "If you have observed negative stereotyping of Arabs on television, you have the advantage over us, inasmuch as we have never been contacted by an Arabian or Arab-American organization to set forth for our edification examples of such stereotyping."

ABC's Julie Hoover denied that ABC was offering viewers a

stereotype image, adding that "any stereotyping of a minority on television may have the effect of reinforcing prejudice, and is, therefore, potentially damaging to an image of a group." ABC attorney Larry Loeb concurred with Hoover, explaining that the network's policies prohibit the slandering "of any individual or group based on the basis of age, color, national origin, race, religion, or sex."

At CBS the former Vice President of Broadcast Standards, Van Gordon Sauter, took a different slant. According to Sauter, stereotypes exist because "the Arab world is considered dramatic and mysterious (an illusion heightened by years of misrepresentation of one form or another in all the mass media), and thus is drawn upon for fictional source material." Sauter's replacement, Donn O'Brien, acknowledged that he had never seen a "good Arab" on TV and that we usually see them as warmongers and/or covetous desert rulers.

Stereotyping does not affect only the Arabs. The motion picture industry gave audiences over 2,000 Hollywood Westerns that presented warped pictures of the Native American.

The racism that led to the internment of Japanese-Americans during World War II was created partly by the motion picture industry, which for years typecast the Oriental as villain, and partly by the press, especially the Hearst newspapers. Fortunately, the yellow peril hysteria, the stereotyping, and the myth are gone.

Thirty years ago there were few black faces on TV. Whenever blacks briefly appeared in minor roles, producers portrayed them as submissive and simpleminded. Note the following excerpt from a letter to *TV Guide* in June, 1959: "Television...is notably lacking in the presentation of Negro performers.... Negro performers are limited to a few songs and dances on the variety shows .... Why can't some of the detective and comedy series work Negroes into their scripts, making them an ordinary part of television life as they are an ordinary part of everyday life?" At the time, producers, writers and network officials had little contact with blacks. But pressure groups and the civil rights movement brought increased sensitivity and change.

Scholars exclude the problem of Arab stereotypes from most major academic works and government documents. One such document is the U.S. Commission on Civil Rights study entitled "Window Dressing on the Set: Women and Minorities in Television," published in 1977. This report, compiled by Helen Loukas, focuses on the stereotyping and lack of representation of minorities and women. It also discusses the effects of such stereotypes on viewers.

I met with Helen Loukas in her Washington office where she told me, "I share your concerns about the portrayal of Arabs on television." Does television play a major role in stereotyping Arabs and other ethnic groups? I asked. "Oh, yes," she said, "not television itself, but all forms of the media. The time people spend with different media is important. And most people spend more time with television." Loukas told me that stereotypes diminish our ability to deal realistically with other human beings. She also explained how a stereotype begins: "At an early age we get a germ of an idea of what people are like. That idea exists for a long period of time and it can become so basic, so deeply felt, that it eventually becomes accepted as the truth." Added Loukas, "You may have a prejudice against certain people, but if accused of that prejudice, you're most likely to deny it."

In the early 70s, in his TV special *Bill Cosby on Prejudice*, the gifted comedian raised a host of questions about the effects of biases. He satirized the stereotyping of nineteen groups, ranging from the Chinese, who, he said, chase only after Western women, to the elderly, who "take up space that others could use." Cosby's performance helped viewers to become more aware of how ridiculous some prejudices appear when openly voiced. He rightfully pointed out how most people, regardless of their nationality, religious beliefs or color are essentially the same. Cosby, however, excluded the Arab from his list of victims.

Cultural assassinations of ethnic groups occur when there exists no documentation of the group to counter fallacious images. For example, a *TV Guide* commentary (June 13, 1981) contends that a "long line of minority groups ... claim that TV has done them wrong .... Indeed, it's hard to find a minority these days that hasn't been maligned on television."

One government report, according to *TV Guide*, claims that women and blacks occupy a "disproportionately high number of demeaning and comical roles." Hispanics, said another study, are all too likely to be depicted as "criminal types." The editors mention other groups that television has treated unfairly: businessmen, blue-collar workers, nurses and senior citizens. Absent from *TV Guide*'s first-rate commentary was the TV Arab.

Until now the image of the TV Arab has been neglected. This documentation of images, however, should help bring about needed awareness and change. In the course of writing this book, I did meet with network officials, writers and producers who said they would be more than willing to correct false Arab stereotypes. In Los Angeles, Cy Chermack, the producer of the popular police show, *CHiPs*, told me. "It bothers me in terms of your children and grandchildren who are

American and who are asked to be proud of their Arab background and culture. They look at the (television) screen and say, 'Daddy, is that us?' And the answer is no."

Part of the problem is that members of the television profession know very few Arabs and their perceptions of the Arab world come not from personal contact but from secondary sources such as motion pictures, newscasts, editorial cartoons, newspaper and magazine articles and other televisions shows. Jack Guss, story editor of *Trapper John, M.D.*, says, "I think that as a writer, the origin of anything I do comes of my human empathy for the character. And that transcends racial and cultural lines. But if I'm not familiar with the culture or the setting, I'm not going to select an Arab as the protagonist or antagonist of my story. I can't relate to it."

Guss says writers are "anxious to deepen characterizations but it's difficult to provide viewers with in-depth characters unless you know the characters."

The importance of educating television writers about Arabs cannot be underestimated. As Virginia Carter, TAT/Tandem vice-president of creative affairs, pointed out, there exists "this propensity in humankind to pick on someone . . . . It's always those whom we don't know (or who appear different) that we hate." She explained that the Japanese image is certainly more positive today than it was twenty-five years ago, and we welcome Japanese investments in this country. "We see them as family. We haven't done that with the Arabs," she said.

I am not suggesting that television writers throw one big Hollywood party and invite only Arabs. But as a group, television writers tend to be a clannish bunch. They live in the same areas of the country and move in the same social circles. Many live in Beverly Hills, which has experienced an influx of wealthy Arab residents in recent years. Yet because of where some Arabs reside, their lifestyles become exaggerated in the television shows their neighbors write.

"It's my impression," said *Bionic Woman* producer Harve Bennett, "since I have property that is surrounded on three sides by Arab buyers, that in Southern California (Arab) investments are huge."

Alan Rafkin, producer of *One Day at a Time*, said that he hears about Arabs from his friends in real estate, "My God, they've bought up another four corners in Beverly Hills."

Rafkin's show *One Day* has included several jokes about Arab wealth and the promiscuity of Arab men. Rafkin's associate, Virginia Carter, told me this material was "rooted in misinformation or lack of information entirely . . . . I have too much respect for the people I work with and myself," she said, "to think that negative images result from malicious undercurrents of conscious hate or dislike."

I agree with Carter in general that the problem is not malicious intent but willful ignorance. I saw this confirmed during a thought-provoking evening I spent at writer Jack Guss' home in Bel Air. Guss was naturally concerned about how his friends, mostly TV writers, would react to my research on stereotypes. During the course of the evening, one of the guests called to say that he was not coming and informed Guss that he felt comfortable with his current perceptions of Arabs.

When the company arrived, we chatted informally over drinks and dinner on the patio. I discovered that nearly all of the eighteen guests thought that Iranians are Arabs. "They might as well be Arabs because they come from the same part of the world," one writer said. One of the more interesting comments came from another writer who worked on the *Six Million Dollar Man* episode, "Deathprobe." He told me that the producer would not allow him to use a Russian heavy, but then, bingo, the producer gave him a green light to use an Arab. That solved the problem.

One woman said she had visited two Arab countries and that her husband never wrote about them in his teleplays. In one country she never left the hotel. Yet she told me that she didn't like the way she saw Arabs living and thought it best not to write "anything good about them. The men," she said, "have too many wives and oppress their women." She said her husband told her the *Koran* sanctions such punishments as cutting off hands at the wrists, and that Moslems are not "humanistic." Perhaps her perceptions of Arabs emanate not from "knowledge" based on personal experiences but "knowledge" acquired from the TV stereotype.

Another writer at the party said he believed all Arab countries are "backward" and equated the word Arab with "oil terrorists." But I told him of my friendship with Sheik Essa of Bahrain, a man who is an intellectual, composer, historian and poet. I took advantage of this opportunity to tell these TV writers about Bahrain, an island about thirteen miles from Saudi Arabia and 150 miles from Iran. The country has a population of 300,000, including 1,000 Americans. In the mid-1930s, Bahrain was the first sheikdom in the Arabian Gulf to discover oil. Today little oil remains. But Bahrain has become a center for tourism and a thriving international market. The future promises more trade. By the late 1980s, an $800 million causeway will link the island with Saudi Arabia.

Bahrain is the most Westernized of the Gulf states. Women, for example, are an integral part of the work force. Still, there are the contrasts that mark all developing Arab countries: men and women in Western dress mingle on the streets with those in traditional Arab garb; potters and tinsmiths work in the shadows of hotel skyscrapers; pollution from an industrial plant stains a mosque. But some things never change, like the Bahraini view of hospitality. The people are courteous and enthusiastic about their country and give special attention to their guests.

Sheik Essa and I first met in 1977 at an afternoon tea for communications specialists. Afterward he gave me a quick tour of Bahrain's radio and TV stations. Bahraini television specials pay tribute to the country's traditions, but also feature contemporary plays and science fiction programs that show the influence of *Star Wars* and *Close Encounters* on that part of the world. Sheik Essa then introduced me to his family. He invited me to dinner at his house with his wife and teenage son. There were over twenty courses, from roast lamb to *baklawa*.

Two historians also joined us for dinner. They discussed how they are preserving the songs of the local pearl divers. Before the Japanese developed cultured pearls, Bahrain enjoyed a thriving pearl industry. Only a few divers are alive today—and all are over seventy years old. The historians are recording the songs they wrote and their way of life. Sheik Essa has passed much time with the divers and is responsible for the effort to preserve the folklore surrounding them.

After informing the writers about this tiny Arab nation, I wanted to know why a program could not be produced on the sheik.

"No," one writer replied. "Nobody would believe it."

Some entertaining television shows have featured sympathetic Arabs. Jack Guss himself wrote one, a 1976 episode of *Medical Center* called "The Price of a Child." The show provides an exception to the tired stereotype by avoiding most cliches. "Child" is about the son of a wealthy Arab ruler who takes parental interest in a fatherless Jewish boy and a romantic interest in the boy's mother. The boy needs an expensive kidney operation and his mother, Esther (Louise Lasser), struggles to support herself and the boy and pay for his medical care by running a kosher deli.

Enter Pete Rashid (Dick Shawn), the wealthy Arab, who happens to be hospitalized at the same time as the boy. *Medical Center*'s protagonist, Dr. Joe Gannon (Chad Everett), jokingly tells Rashid that "when you're on your feet you can buy me a hospital." Shortly afterwards, Gannon's supervisor tells him, "Some lunatic wants to buy the Medical Center so he can give it away as a gift."

A scene such as this, of course, plays up the stereotype. But other scenes show Rashid as a man of feeling, with a sense of humor. He is not a one-dimensional character. Rashid eventually falls in love with Esther. But Rashid's more traditional father hopes to circumvent any impending marriage. Love triumphs and "Child" concludes on a happy note. Rashid's father turns out to be somewhat backward but rather protective, afraid that his son might be hurt and used by Esther. He soon recognizes Esther is a good woman and accepts her. Esther, who previously had flattered Rashid only because she needed money for her own operation, comes to truly love this compassionate man.

Guss said of the drama, "There is mutual respect at the show's conclusion, which I think is important, and most shows have not shown that." He said he could not recall seeing another program portray an Arab character as positively.

"You know, I would love to see this problem solved," he added.

Guss said that he did not wish to demean current television writers but explained that "what dominates television is a common denominator. If this country had an ethnic balance of—let's say eighty percent blacks and twenty percent whites—there would be a lot more soul music, a lot more black programming . . . if the Arab population of this country was larger, they would be getting a helluva lot of attention. It's sad when any culture doesn't have an opportunity to express its pride when they're watching television," Guss said.

He pointed out that if more Americans of Arab descent worked in television, "there would have to be a better balance because they would be conscious of the kind of laziness that goes into making characterizations of their own people."

"Jack," he said, "I really believe anything works. Look at Vic Tayback. In *Alice*, viewers think of Vic as a guy who runs a diner, who enjoys women, a beer and a good laugh. But nobody sees him as an Arab-American. But if Vic were to be an Arab figure," said Guss, "representing Arab culture, that would be a very positive thing."

"Until recently I don't think I ever saw a good Indian," he said. "I grew up when Indians were the heavies in movie series; they were always yelling and scalping women. It wasn't until we became socially conscious that the Indians were a people, with a history and a culture, that we came to respect them.

"It's certainly possible to have a comedy about Arabs. Throw in all the stereotypes, like *Barney Miller*, you know? The crazies show up and there is no distinction between the criminals and the cops. And it's kind of wonderful to see."

Guss had foresight, for not long after our conversation *Barney Miller* featured two older men, Haddad the Arab and Kotterman the Jew, in an excellent two-part program, "Homicide." Writers Frank Dungan and Jeff Stein humanize rather than dehumanize our perceptions of two Semitic cousins, Haddad and Kotterman.

"There are more Jews in the industry than there are Arabs," said *One Day* producer Alan Rafkin, "so naturally we do more Jewish stories. Sure, if Arabs were producing, writing and directing a lot of shows, you'd see more about Arabs ... if we had an Arab working on *One Day*, he might say, 'Excuse me, Alan, we're not all rich. We don't all do the same things'."

If would be helpful, as Rafkin suggests, to include Arab-Americans in television's work force. But a more meaningful change is necessary. The TV industry relies on repeatable formats with repeatable villains. As producer Harve Bennett said, Arabs make particularly delectable "heavies."

TV's formats are highly simplistic and lead to the portrayal of good guys and bad guys. Both writer Irving Pearlberg and producer Bennett told me they believe *television does not portray any ethnic group fairly.* Arabs are singled out, said Bennett, because "there's an energy crisis, the activities in Iran are confused with the Arab world and (there is) a general sense of pro-Israeli support" in the U.S.

"I find myself and our country, your country and my country, threatened by the Arab world," said Cy Chermack. "I find Israel, a country to which I have strong emotional ties, threatened by the Arab world as I see it."

Chermack suggested that Arab-Americans interested in bettering their television image might concentrate on getting writers to do more shows that deal with Arab-Americans, since a sympathetic Arab-American might be more believable to audiences at this time than a "good" Arab sheik. Yet consider this: NBC's Jerome Stanley says there is a problem in portraying Arab-Americans on television. They are not easily identifiable, he says, unless they appear in exotic settings and wear robes and headdresses. Viewers can easily identify Hispanics, Jews and other ethnic groups by their surnames; they can identify Orientals by sight. But Stanley contends that viewers won't necessarily recognize Arab names. Stanley makes my point more beautifully than I could. If Arab-Americans are not easily identifiable, it is because we look and act no differently than other Americans.

Alan Rafkin suggested that Arab-Americans should approach the networks and say, "We just want you to know who we are. That's all. We want you to know that we work for Ford, we work at Yellowstone, and we are doctors, lawyers and clergy. We would like you to see what we are so that you can show the rest of the world, show our children."

Other shows have featured ethnic heroes: *Hill Street Blues*, Italian, Jewish and Hispanic-Americans; *Banacek*, a Polish-American; *Kojak*, a Greek-American; and *Shaft*, a black. Why can't there be a series that features an Arab-American character? We have already explored the possibilities that exist with the character of Mel in *Alice*.

Most of the television executives I interviewed agreed that Arab-Americans need a lobby in Hollywood. During the 1959-60 TV season, producers and writers did a great disservice to another ethnic group, the Italians, with the series *The Untouchables*. The show starred Robert Stack as Treasury agent Eliot Ness and typecast Italian-Americans as gangsters. The Italian-American League and other groups protested that most of the criminals in the series had Italian surnames. About a year after the program debuted, the production company, Desilu, agreed that "there would be no more fictional hoodlums with Italian names" and that the writers would place more emphasis on Nick Rossi, Ness' right-hand man, and the contributions that Italians have made to American culture.

The Italian-American League's efforts led to a diversification of villains. By 1963, the last year of the series, most ethnic groups had been featured. Even the Russians appeared as hoods. One criminal was named Joe Vodka. "Any minority group that has achieved anything has done it through organized pressure," said writer Pearlberg. "The Jews, the blacks, the gays, and the Chicanos a little," he added. Pearlberg said anything short of the applied pressure approach would prove ineffective. But whom to apply pressure on? The production companies? "A production company which has three shows on the air one year could be out the next," he says. Pearlberg also rules out the Writer's Guild and the directors. "Most members of the Writer's Guild would be automatically sympathetic toward members of any race;" and directors, he said, "direct what is written for them." Rather, Pearlberg advises, "Go to the top, to the networks, because whatever pressure they exert goes downward and would affect everything. You should get to a point where a broadcast standards division of any network will say, 'No, we won't accept any reference to camel jockey.' Or if they will tell producers, 'We will not accept anything that can legitimately be construed as anti-Arab.' If that could be done, then I think the battle is more than half-won."

CBS's Broadcast Standards official in New York, James Baerg, described the role of the standards division as viewing "material at various stages of production," noting that his area is "involved with the program while it is still in script form." Said Baerg: "While we oversee it, we do not produce it." He believes that the Arab stereotype "is attractive" because "it is an easy thing to do; it's the thing that is going to be more readily accepted by a large number of the audience. It is the same as throwing in sex and violence when an episode is slow," Baerg said.

Don Bay, Tom Kersey's associate at ABC, also described the role assigned to the broadcast standards division. Bay explained that what happens with entertainment programs is that "after the script is written, after the talks have taken place between the programming department and the writers, this germ of an idea then goes to the producer. There are discussions in the programming department, then it arrives on our doorstep," said Bay. He pointed out that by the time a show arrives at broadcast standards it is fairly well fixed, a *fait accompli*. "At that point we try to make cosmetic changes," he said, and "to some extent we are successful—in many cases, less so."

NBC's Jerome Stanley suggested that more time be spent meeting with the creators of TV shows, saying they were the ones who needed to be reached with information about Arab stereotypes. Added Stanley: "I think it's human nature to have some underlying prejudice. 'He's different from me and therefore he's not like I am and therefore he's done something wrong'." Stanley equates the TV Arab image of today with yesterday's film image of the Native American.

Right now the Arab remains a favorite whipping boy.

Syndicated columnist Nicholas Von Hoffman has said in the Washington *Post*: "No national, religious or cultural group ... has been so massively and consistently vilified (as the Arabs)."

The editors of *The New Republic* wrote: "Arabs have been the victims of ugly racial stereotyping in recent years; that the standards of what is considered to be respectable in portraying or commenting upon ethnic or national groups apply to Arabs as well as to any others; and ... the widespread casual violation of such standards threatens all potential victims of racial slurs. It ought to stop."

It *hasn't* stopped.

Fairness is sacrificed when producers and writers go into a series with preconceived ideas about people. As we know, notorious Arabs do not appear in a single series, but they are scattered among numerous programs. As far back as the spy spoof series of the 1960s, *The Man From U.N.C.L.E.* and *The Girl From U.N.C.L.E.*, the theme of the Arab as slaver/chauvinist prevailed. In *Man*, Arabs seek to sell David McCallum to a "Jordanian" slave market. In *Girl*, an overly passionate sheik attempts to seduce Stephanie Powers.

TV Arabs still prowl across the tube.

In *Hart to Hart*, Arab dignitaries try to assassinate their king.

In *Charlie's Angels*, Arab terrorists attempt to murder an Arab delegation as well as scores of innocent Americans.

In *The Powers of Matthew Star*, Mr. Moustafa tries to buy the services of kidnapped American geniuses.

In *Simon & Simon*, A.J. reluctantly poses as a Kuwaiti oil sheik with eight wives.

In *Small and Frye*, the detectives jeer: "You can tell the man's an Arab. He stole the bedsheets from the Aladdin Hotel."

In *Soap*, a character suffers from heart problems because her "daughter is dating a PLO member."

In *Friday Night Videos*, as The Clash sings "Rock the Casbah," an Arab strides around America, behaving as though he owns the country.

In *The Greatest American Hero*, "Hero" breaks up an "Arab oil cartel."

In *Callahan*, Arabs threaten to "shut off" American's oil supply.

In *Lou Grant*, a detective argues that Arab oil is America's oil. "The Arabs would still be riding their camels over it if it weren't for us," he says.

In *Dynasty*, Blake Carrington shouts: Do I "have to invade the damn (Arab) country to get my oil out?"

In *Masquerade*, an "International Arab Army terrorist" holds fourteen Americans hostage.

In *Airwolf*, Arabs bring about the destruction of a destroyer, killing hundreds of innocent Americans.

In addition to these shows and the programs discussed in previous chapters, I have also documented Arab stereotypes in TV specials such as *The Ninja, The Pirate, The 700 Club Telethon* (1984), *Lace, Scruples* and in regular weekly shows: *The Feather and Father Gang, Sweepstakes, Get Smart, Happy Days Again, Wonder Woman, Sha Na Na, Skag, The Muppet Show, Barbara Mandrell, Sanford and Son, Forever Fernwood, Harper Valley P.T.A., The American Girls, Doctor Who, Hawaii Five-O* and *All That Glitters.* There have also been cases in which well-known personalities have made derogatory statements about Arabs on *To Tell the Truth* and *Phil Donahue.*

Openness to change is an American tradition and the strength of our society. I believe that creators of television programs will replace the stereotype with a fairer image. Viewers could then see more positive and realistic characterizations of Arabs on television. Such redress would reveal a people just as radiantly human as all others who grace and enrich our lives on this marvelously varied earth.

There have been some signs of progress. After my interviews in California, I went to New York to meet with Bettye King Hoffmann, NBC's vice president of program information resources. She showed me a copy of a report that specifically requested the producers of *Joe's World* (a series that has not aired as of this writing) to "please delete derogatory reference to Arabs and the line 'two-bit camel jockeys'."

CBS's Vice President of Broadcast Standards Donn O'Brien told me of a script for a *Barnaby Jones* segment which originally included Arab characters involved in a white slavery ring. When the show finally aired, the culprits could not be identified by country or heritage.

"It worked just as well without the Arab heavies," O'Brien said.

"We don't want to contaminate the public's perception of people here or abroad. So you don't show Arab white-slavers—at all," said O'Brien's predecessor, Van Gordon Sauter, who is now vice president of the CBS Broadcast Group. Sauter added: "That's something you don't do because it's representative of nothing—of a myth that is no longer tolerable in a hopefully enlightened society . . . . I would like to think that a CBS program would not say, 'Ah, we need a villain. Let's send out for some Middle East costumes right away.' That's not tolerable, not acceptable."

It is not tolerable, not acceptable because television's depictions are more than mere froth. Communications scholar Professor Erik Barnouw has said that television is "the definer and transmitter of a society's values. Viewers feel they understand from television what's going on in the world. They unconsciously look to it for guidance as to what is important, good and desirable and what is not."

"Entertainment plays a leading role in shaping attitudes and ideas, including political ideas," writes Barnouw. And entertainment programs can act "as effective propaganda, precisely because they are received, as something else—entertainment," he says.

"The aura surrounding the word is important," writes Barnouw, because entertainment is a "word associated with relaxation . . . a word that lulls our critical facilities. We speak of our popular (television) fiction as 'mere' entertainment, which means it is assumed to be without messages. But behind this mere entertainment lie, inevitably, unspoken premises, which we are maneuvered into accepting."

A 1983 study by the American Enterprise Institute in Washington, D.C. shows that two out of three television writers and producers "believe that TV entertainment should be a major force for social reform." Television's creators "are not in it for the money. They also seek to move their audience toward their own vision of the good society."

Producer Norman Lear has said: "We have learned that more people will absorb information when it is couched in entertainment. And the higher the entertainment level of the show, the bigger the audience and the more successful the show."

Lear explains how television programs transmit social messages: "When *Starsky and Hutch* went on the air, there was one scene when they got in their car and used seat belts. Within the next six days, maybe 100,000 people bought seat belts. When Fonz on *Happy Days* went in and got a library card, something like 500,000 people went in and got library cards."

I believe that most TV producers subscribe to the philosophy of Norman Lear, who said: "Television is very powerful; I hope we can use it constructively."

But TV is not constructive when people are denigrated. Stereotypes cause us to form "pictures in our heads," a phrase made famous by Walter Lippmann almost sixty years ago. These pictures may cause us to view others not as humans but as caricatures.

We should remember that stereotyping is not a modern phenomenon. Nor should we assume that stereotypes cannot be eradicated.

In the Bible, for example, we find a parable of the good Samaritan, whose people in Biblical days were stereotyped as villains. The parable forever eliminated that stereotype.

A revolutionary thought at that time and place—the idea that a *good* Samaritan exists. So astonishing was this impression that the meaning of the word *Samaritan* was completely reversed. Today, Samaritan is synonymous with goodness and compassion.

The time has come to retire "The Instant Arab TV Kit." Viewers should see balanced presentations, with Arabs as people who are friendly and honest folk common to the human species. Writers and producers are conscious of their power to influence public perceptions. If they were to show Arabs as they really are, viewers would not be so quick to see them as billionaires, bombers and belly dancers. Producers could dispatch this stereotype to video purgatory, to join other worn-out stereotypes—the black domestic, the savage Indian, the cunning Oriental and the Italian mobster—never to reach the screen again.

Dispelling a Stereotype

This book documents the stereotype, counters myths and encourages a more balanced image of the Arab. To avoid exposing the reader to one long bleat, dozens of additional stereotying examples are excluded.

Now what about solutions to the problem? What might be done to correct this lopsided image? Does writing a book and revealing the offenses and the offenders suffice? After all, "TV stereotypes everybody," says Andrew Mills, *TV Guide*'s assistant managing editor.

Yet network policies "prohibit the broadcast of material that demeans or is derogatory to any racial, religious, or ethnic group." Alice M. Henderson, **CBS** vice president of broadcast standards, West Coast, has written, "There is no intent by CBS . . . to unfavorably stereotype individuals of any ethnic origin. . . . We take seriously our commitment that programming broadcast on the **CBS** Television Network should meet high standards of acceptability." NBC-TV's Broadcast Standards and Practices manual states: "Television programs should reflect a wide range of roles for all people . . . and should endeavor to depict men, women and children in a positive manner, *keeping in mind always the importance of dignity to every human being*" (emphasis added).

Network guidelines notwithstanding, the medium, as Mills says, does indeed stereotype everybody. In the past, viewers even witnessed Viet Nam veterans portrayed as violence-prone drug addicts or psychological misfits with sexual problems. Eventually TV professionals became sensitized to this false image of veterans and took appropriate action—the stereotype disappeared.

Stereotyping, whether intentional or unintentional, is not the American way. When one ethnic or minority group is degraded, for whatever reason, we all suffer.

As for the Arab image, how would Jewish-Americans react if they witnessed a host of TV Shylocks posing as nuclear terrorists? Would blacks welcome being portrayed as white-slavers? Would Hispanics be chagrined if they were shown, along with Orientals, as crude foreigners buying up America? Would educated Western women remain silent if depicted as submissive harem chattels?

Benjamin Franklin advised, "To get the bad Customs of a Country chang'd and new ones, though better, introduc'd, it is necessary first to remove the Prejudices of the People, enlighten their Ignorance, and convince them that their Interest will be promoted by the propos'd Changes; and this is *not the work of a Day*."

Franklin's words take on added meaning when we consider stereotypes. Black Americans appealed for over sixty years before motion picture executives took their grievances seriously and began addressing the black stereotype.

Does an absence of will to attack the stereotype exist? How long will it take before TV writers and producers begin to address this issue? Some will take positive action. Others will not. In Los Angeles and New York, most of the men and women interviewed were fair-minded. One-third of those interviewed expressed pro-Israeli feelings. Such feelings could account for some negative Arab images. One producer, Cy Chermack, accused me of working with the Saudis. Another producer, Meta Rosenberg, said that she didn't care about Arabs and considered the Arab-American community to be "insignificant." During a few of the interviews, I felt like a black defending himself and his heritage against members of the Ku Klux Klan.

Another one-third of the interviewees were neutral.

The remaining third were sincerely troubled and concerned about the stereotype.

Writer Irving Pearlberg, whose "good" TV Arab in *Police Woman* became half-French, told me that "most Americans know little about real-life Arabs and that the little they do know comes from television." This is significant since most television executives know just as little about Arabs as the rest of the American public.

Pearlberg said: "Forty percent of TV writers are Jewish. But no Jewish writer," he added, "would deliberately present an unbalanced picture in which Arabs were more villainous than they were heroic. If anything, most of the Jewish writers I know would bend over backwards to go the other way."

In his critical work, *The View From Sunset Boulevard*, Ben Stein said: "A distinct majority, especially of the writers of situation comedies, is Jewish." According to Stein, "TV people have certain likes (of people who are harmless) and dislikes (of people and groups who are rivals), and these likes and dislikes are translated into television programming. In turn, this problem raises the public acceptance of the favored groups and the public dislike of the resented groups."

Stein perceives TV professionals as a homogenized mass.

I do not. I do believe, consciously or subconsciously, that "TV people" favor Jews over Arabs. Seldom do we see Jewish villains on television. We experience Jewish culture and heroics, not because of a "Zionist conspiracy," but because Jewish-Americans who work in the profession rightly refuse to denigrate themselves or their heritage. A conspiracy isn't necessary to continue the cycle of stereotyping—complacency is enough.

Is stereotyping a propagandist's tool?

Consider Irwin Shaw's *Evening in Byzantium*, a four-hour TV special. The novel was adapted for television by Glen A. Larson and Michael Sloan.

Shaw's novel, which sold over one million copies, is a touching love story about an old man in love with a younger woman. Arabs are not mentioned. But the TV special, which attracted over twenty million viewers, focused on the Arab-as-crude and the Arab-as-terrorist.

The TV version featured a nuclear terrorist group called the PLF (note the resemblance of PLF to PLO). The PLF murders scores of innocent people in a Cannes movie theatre. And the PLF blows up several passenger planes en route to the United States. PLF "terrorists" also prepare to drop nuclear bombs on Washington, D.C., New York and Los Angeles.

Byzantium also features three oil-rich sheiks that want to make a movie. They seek to portray Israelis as nuclear terrorists. No way, says *Byzantium*'s protagonist; such a film would be blatant propaganda. But can't Larson and Sloan's adaptation of *Byzantium* be called propaganda? Would the writers slant the special in such a way that viewers would perceive Israelis, not Arabs, as terrorists?

Larson and several other noted TV producers refused to grant interviews: Aaron Spelling, Leonard Goldberg (*Hart to Hart, Charlie's Angels* and others), Howard Koch (*The Pirate*). But broadcast standards personnel were always accessible.

Why don't Arab-Americans work with broadcast standards officials? And why aren't they writing and producing teleplays? Couldn't their presence help to provide a needed balance? For years, Orientals, Hispanics, blacks, women and others sought representation. Such representation could ensure equitable treatment. How could one stereotype a friend or colleague? As producer Alan Rafkin said, "If Arabs were producing, writing and directing a lot of shows, you'd see more about Arabs."

According to those men and women I interviewed, the Arab image in the programs cited here did not involve a broadcast standards official or a TV writer/producer of Arab descent. Virginia Carter, TAT/ Tandem's vice president of creative affairs, best summarizes the situation: "I don't know anyone in the industry that's an Arab-American."

Several months after my interview with Tom Kersey, ABC's vice-president of broadcast standards, he wrote: "I regret to report that we still spend most of our time rejecting Arab stereotypes/ridicule, thus, rather than changing the character to positive representations the producers and writers simply drop the character and Arabs per se disappear from the television screen. There have been exceptions of course, but very few."

Does one offset negative images by throwing in Arabs when "an episode is slow?" Or by having "Arabs per se disappear from the television screen?" Hasn't the medium matured to a point where Arab characters can be presented in depth and with care? Don't viewers observe as much?

Ignorance about Arab-Americans does not excuse the stereotype. To counter past images, writers could focus on typical Americans of Arab descent, just as they focus on other Americans of Italian, Polish, Mexican or Jewish descent. Inserting positive Arab-American characters is a simple task.

Viewers learned to identify with a heroic black, Mr. T, in *The A Team*. And with an intelligent rabbi in the *Lanigan's Rabbi* series. And with the fascinating Rhoda Morgenstern in *Rhoda*. The *Bridget Loves Bernie* series concerned a poor Jewish boy who married a rich Irish girl. The *Chico and the Man* series focused on two men from radically different cultural backgrounds—a Mexican-American and a white garage owner. The men grew to respect each other, but some Mexican-Americans criticized *Chico* because no Chicanos appeared. Producer James Komack soon added minorities to the cast.

The Arab-American community could help combat the stereotype by informing producers and writers about people of the Middle East, their history and culture. Informed individuals are more apt to correct the stereotype than those who are not so informed.

Arab-Americans could consider the following:

*Emulate action taken by other American groups—blacks,

Hispanics, Jews and Italians. When Arab stereotypes appear, seek out the expertise and support of Arab-American and other ethnic and minority organizations.

*TV professionals could meet with Arab-Americans. They could attend social events such as picnics, conventions, weddings, mother-daughter and father-son banquets and church and mosque gatherings.

*Conferences on the stereotype could be offered at selected universities. Speakers could include Arab-Americans of various professions. Members of broadcast standards and those TV creators who have debunked the stereotype, as well as those who continue to demean Arabs, could also attend. Such conferences could promote thought and discussion, and perhaps bring about a more balanced image. Programs which contain Arab stereotypes could be offered. To place the stereotype in perspective, members of other minority/ethnic groups should also participate.

*Encourage Middle East nations to invite TV professionals to visit the area. Expose TV people over there to TV people over here. Such exposure can only result in a better understanding of the Arab people. Such exposure could also bring co-production ventures to fruition.

*"In the early years of this century," writes syndicated columnist Nick Thimmesch, "the Jews were an abused and discriminated against people in this country." Yesterday's Jews were despised as exemplars of modernism. Today's Arabs are depicted as purveyors of primitivism. To wipe out the current stereotype, Thimmesch suggests that Arab-Americans peruse *Not the Work of A Day,* published by the Anti-Defamation League of B'nai B'rith. *Work Of A Day* documents how American Jews countered their stereotype.

No better guideline for television professionals is more consistent with the American character than the words of John Stuart Mill: "Not the violent conflict between parts of the truth," Mill said, "but the quiet suppression of half of it, is the formidable evil; there is always hope when people are forced to listen to both sides; it is when they attend to one that errors harden into prejudices, and truth itself ceases to have the effect of truth, by being exaggerated into falsehood."

To prevent truth from "being exaggerated into falsehood," TV's creators could consider the following:

*Study those all-too-obvious myths noted here and counter them.

*Reveal unfair Arab stereotypes in a documentary, titled *Misunderstanding Arabia.* Use the telling CBS documentary, *Misunderstanding China,* as a model.

*In comedy shows, let viewers occasionally laugh *with* Arab characters, not only *at* them. For example, when one of my Arab students at the university was called a "camel jockey," he simply smiled. He then faced his harasser and said: "You know, the first time I ever saw a camel was here—at the St. Louis zoo."

*Feature the heritage of Arab-Americans, such as Jamie Farr of *After MASH* and Vic Tayback of *Alice.*

*In a series such as *Cheers,* viewers could see Carla date an Arab, or an American with Arab roots. The customers chide her for going out with a nomad or a sheik. Carla counters by saying: "He's a guy—just like you guys. He likes me. And I like him."

*In police and detective shows, writers could show Arabs lurking in shadows and being cunning—in the name of law and order. Have Arab-Americans work with *Simon & Simon, The A Team, Remington Steele* or *Matt Houston.* Couldn't the producers of *Hill Street Blues* feature an Arab-American as an integral part of Capt. Frank Furillo's ethnically diverse team of crime-busters?

One constructive step toward altering the stereotype is focusing on children's programming. Over the years my children and those of other Arab-Americans witnessed only distorted self-images on cartoon shows. They are not the only group whose children suffer from the pain of ethnic stereotyping. Other groups have been exploited in the name of entertainment.

Television's professionals have been correcting past injustices. In 1976 the first episode of an animated cartoon series, *Jabberjaw,* featured an Oriental villain, drawn like a Fu Manchu stereotype. Two years later, ABC-TV introduced a courageous Asian, Samurai, to integrate its extra-terrestrial superheroes force. Unlike the bad Fu Manchu, Samurai represents good.

"For years Asians have been typecast as leaders of Oriental evil, or unthinking subservients to Anglo justice and intelligence," writes Dr. Charles Cheng of U.C.L.A. Concerned about the Asian cartoon image, Dr. Cheng met with ABC officials. This meeting and others led the network to create the Samurai hero. Network executives also encouraged Asian-Americans to discuss the overall treatment of Asians in cartoon shows.

"Broadcasting to children is the very beginning of the learning experience," said ABC's Tom Kersey. That being the case, American children, including those of Arab descent, should be spared the denial of their dignity. I do not want my children's children to cringe when watching the Fonz humiliate "Abdul'O the Un-Cool'O." Nor should they flinch when the superfriends collar the Arab heavies.

Instead, children should see programs that feature Arab cartoon heroes who pal around with the Fonz and the superfriends. Let's see the Fonz and "Abdul'O the *Cool'O*" work together. As a team. If the superfriends say it's neat to be friends with an Arab, who's to argue?

Or create a series based on *Fat Albert and the Cosby Kids*. Call it *Fat Omar and the Shaheen Kids*. But treat the Shaheens the same way you treat the Cosbys.

TV Guide reporter Neil Hickey has written that the ultimate TV accomplishment is "to catch the child's imagination by showing him the world, what its possibilities are, how people get along in it, how they interact with each other, and what his (her) place in it might be." Hickey explained that positive role models are essential. He emphasized that all children need folk heroes.

In their early years, children absorb a general set of cultural values. Dr. Edward Palmer of the Children's Television Workshop has said: "I suspect that TV informs and instructs in its own way as much as colleges do. *TV has a greater influence than all the formal establishments devoted to education*" (emphasis added).

"American children of Arab descent should be given a positive image, just like our black and our Asian children," said producer Cy Chermack. "They should see positive portrayals of themselves on television. And I would support that. I would support that on our show (*CHiPs*). And I would support that in any public service program or any other way I could," Chermack said.

TV helps shape our morality. Old stereotypes never fade-to-black; they just fade into syndication.

An effective antidote to the entertainment paraphernalia—camels, Cadillacs, black tents, oil wells, harem dancers, sheiks and terrorists—may be found in TV documentaries, especially those PBS documentaries narrated, produced, written and directed by Jo Franklin-Trout, a former producer of the *MacNeil-Lehrer Report*.

Two three-hour series', *Saudi Arabia* (1982) and *The Oil Kingdoms* (1983), are video textbooks by Franklin-Trout—entertaining and informative programs that provide a penetrating analysis of Arab history—from the birth of Islam to instant oil riches. The six programs provide a balanced and incisive view of Saudi Arabia, Oman, Kuwait, Qatar, the United Arab Emirates and Bahrain. The documentaries bring fairness to areas where ignorance has nurtured biases.

Franklin-Trout contends that "you cannot ever understand a people or a country or their subsequent actions unless you understand their history." Her documentaries steer deftly around the stereotype. A Middle East official tells her: "Today's Saudis 'don't want their son to be a noble savage,' they want him to go to Stanford." Notes Franklin-Trout: "There are more American Ph.D.s in the Saudi Arabian cabinet than there are in the U.S. Cabinet."

As an American woman in the Middle East, Franklin-Trout first thought that Arab women "are far behind us when it comes to civil rights and freedom. But in fact when you take into account their history ... what you're struck with is how far, how fast they have moved," she said.

"They actually have removed some restrictions, such as allowing women in certain occupations, that took us many more years in the United States. I, for one, graduated from college in 1968, and at that time in the U.S. there were almost no women doctors ... and women were not allowed on the air to do news because who would believe the news of a woman? I got my first job in television because the Civil Rights Act forced the networks, for the first time, to put a woman on the air doing the news."

Franklin-Trout noted that in Saudi Arabia there are more women physicians than there are men, although women treat only women patients. The country is still a highly segregated society.

Arabs of the Gulf nations shared with her a common anxiety—how to achieve progress without sacrificing cherished traditional beliefs. A Saudi official asks: "Why continue to try and accomplish in five or six years what other nations accomplished in 20 or 30 years?" He wonders how all-too-rapid progress may affect the family.

The producer-writer has said that the months she spent on location gave her a greater sense of the importance of family, families in general and her own husband and two children in particular. "In the Arab world, the family is extended—it is the most important element of life," she said.

Franklin-Trout's documentaries are remarkable achievements that touch the mind and the heart. She humanizes the men and women of six Middle Eastern nations. Various points of view are considered during the reporting, filming and assembly of her programs. Hard facts take precedence over catchy phrases. And the interviews resemble not inquisitions but concern for individual rights. Because of her documentaries, the people are much less an exotic mystery than ever before.

Ed Bradley has said that this book will be "a valuable passport to objectivity in the future treatment of the Arab." And ABC's Tom Kersey told me: "One of the most sincere promises this department can make is the inclusion of minorities in positive portrayals in all of our programming.''

In October 1983, Kersey sent me a copy of a treatment for a forthcoming TV special. Kersey sought out my advice about equitable images concerning Palestinian and Israeli portraits. Such action on the part of ABC-TV's Office of Broadcast Standards and Practices is commendable and invites cautious optimism.

Perceptions of a better world are not abstract but are always derived from personal experience. During the summer of 1983, I joined a gathering in Clairton, twenty miles up the Monongahela River from Pittsburgh. Four generations of Americans with Arab roots mingled at a park pavilion. This reunion brought back memories of those early immigrants who gave so much of themselves to us. Not material things. Love of one's fellow man, love of family, love of God.

"What you learn from home always stays with you," were my mother, Nazara's, words. "You may forget for a while. But you will always come back to your roots."

That summer was memorable for another reason. My wife, Bernice, had recovered from a heart attack. She was treated at the St. Louis Jewish Hospital by a Swiss-American doctor. Her roommate, Ruth Goldstein, also had an attack. Ruth is a Jewish-American. Bernice, a Palestinian-American. In the hospital they comforted each other. They are now friends.

To some, universal brotherhood seems unattainable. But Khalil Gibran believed that by respecting one's fellow man we learn to respect ourselves.

"You are my brother and I love you. I love you worshipping in your church, kneeling in your temple, or praying in your mosque. You and I and all our children are of one religion, for the varied paths of religion are but the fingers of the loving hand of the supreme being, extended to all, offering completeness of spirit to all, anxious to receive it."

In Clairton's steel mills I shared sweat with men of many ethnic backgrounds. Mutual respect prevailed. Steelworkers can wipe out stereotypes. So can writers and producers.

Chapter Notes

IN SEARCH OF THE ARABS

[1]Beginning with the 1975-76 TV season the author has documented Arab stereotypes. Each year stereotypes appear in approximately 12 new programs. Programs are usually repeated once during the season. The programs then move into syndication where they are again telecast. Many independent and network-affiliated stations air dated cartoon shows and other old programs that feature Arab images. These programs date back to the 1950s (*Captain Gallant of the Foreign Legion*) and the 1960s (*The Man From U.N.C.L.E.* and *The Beverly Hillbillies*). Also, some of the people interviewed have changed jobs. They are identified by the positions they held at the time of the interviews.

[2]Statement on the number of TV receivers made by Norman Fleishman, West Coast director of the Center for Popular Opinions. See "Fighting Forces of Goodness," by John J. Archibald, St. Louis *Post-Dispatch*, Nov. 28, 1980, p. 3D.

[3]For additional information on network "censors" see the "Censors in Action" by Eric Levin in *TV Guide*, Dec. 10, pp. 4-10, and Dec. 17, 1977, pp. 18-22. Also, see "Network Nexus: TV's Guardians of Taste," by David Grunwald, in *The American Way*, American Airlines magazine, June, 1977, pp. 48-51.

[4]For more information on the number of households in the U.S. with TV sets see Len Riley, "All White or All-American?" in *Emmy* magazine, Spring 1980, pp. 30-36.

[5]For more information concerning Dr. George Gerbner's views on stereotyping see *Media Portrayal of the Elderly: Hearings Before the Select Committee on Aging, House of Representatives*, Los Angeles, California, March 26, 1980. Comm. Pub. No. 96-231, U.S. Govt. Printing Office, Washington, 1980.

[6]See Shelley Slade, "The Image of the Arab in America: Analysis of a Poll on American Attitudes," in *The Middle East Journal*, Spring 1981, pp. 143-162.

[7]See Meg Greenfield, "Our Ugly-Arab Complex," in *Newsweek*, Dec. 5, 1977, p. 110.

[8]For an elaboration on Arab contributions see John R. Hayes, editor, *The Genius of Arab Civilization* (New York University Press, 1975), and *ARAMCO and Its World*, edited by Nawwab, Speers and Hoye (ARAMCO: Washington 1980).

[9]See Russell Baker, "Pillowed in Araby," The New York *Times*, May 26, 1979, p. 19.

[10]See Steve Bell, "American Journalism: Heritage Practices, Constraints and Middle East Reportage," in *The American Media and the Arabs*, edited by Hudson and Wolfe (Center for Contemporary Arab Studies at Georgetown University: Washington, 1980), pp. 51-58.

[11]See Ben Hecht, *A Guide for the Bedevilled* (C. Scribner's, New York, 1944).

[12]See John Law, *Arab Investors: Who They Are, What They Buy and Where: Vol. I* (Chase World Information Corporation: New York, 1980). See also Laventhal and Horwath's *Perspective* (Winter 1980). In this issue Benjamin Benson discusses in his article "The Selling of America," U.S. Govt. reports on foreign investments.

[13]See Edward J. Byng, *The World of the Arabs* (Little Brown: Boston, 1944).

[14]See Sari Nasir, *The Arabs and the English* (Longman: London, 1979).

[15]See *Time* magazine, Oct. 11, 1982, pp. 34-64. See also former President Carter's book, *Keeping Faith* (Bantam: New York, 1982).

[16]See Grace Halsell, *Journey to Jerusalem* (Macmillan: New York, 1981).

[17]Main offices of Rotary and Lion's Clubs provided author with the number of Club chapters in the Middle East.

[18]See "Trade Group Meets U.S. Businessmen" by Ron Devren in *Saudi Business*, June 19, 1981, p. 21. And see also "Saudi Arabia in 1973-1983: Ten Years of Progress," in *Newsweek*, May 30, 1983. And "Saudi Jackpot" in *Time*, May 11, 1981. See also "Foreign Direct Investment in the United States in 1982," by William K. Chung and Gregory G. Fouch, in *Survey of Current Business*, August 1983, pp. 31-41.

[19]Letter to author from Robert A. Cornell, Deputy Assistant Secretary for Trade and Investment, Dept. of Treasury, Dec. 19, 1983.

[20]See "The Kingdom and The Power," in *Time*, August 22, 1983.

[21]See "Partners in Growth," in *ARAMCO World Magazine*, January-February, 1977.

CHILDREN AND TEENS

[1]See "Today's Children Listen More to TV than Teachers," in *The Christian Science Monitor*, Oct. 17, 1983, p. 7.

[2]See "Prejudice Still Strong in the U.S.," The St. Louis *Globe-Democrat*, Nov. 16, 1983, p. 10A.

[3]See "The Societal Curriculum and the School Curriculum: Allies or Antagonists?" by Carlos Cortes, in *Journal of Educational Leadership*, April, 1979.

[4]See *The Social Animal*, by Elliott Aronson (W.H. Freeman and Co.: San Francisco, 1972).

[5]See *Media Portrayal of the Elderly: Hearings Before the Select Committee on Aging, House of Representatives*, April 26, 1980, Los Angeles, Calif. (Comm. Pub. No. 96-231—U.S. Govt. Printing Office, Washington, 1980).

[6]See "What the Negro Wants From TV," by Art Peters, in *TV Guide: The First Twenty-Five Years*, edited by Jay S. Harris (New American Library: New York, 1980).

[7]See American-Arab Discrimination Committee Issue Number Two titled *The Influence of the Arab Stereotype on American Children*, introduction by Dr. James Zogby (Washington, 1981).

[8]For additional information concerning Dr. Hitti's remarks regarding Arab women see "Orientalism and Arab Women," by Rosemary Sayigh, in *Arab Studies Quarterly*, Vol. 3, No. 3, Fall 1981).

[9]See *Arabian Sands* by Wilfred Thesiger (Dutton: New York, 1959).

[10]See ABSCRAM in *Sports Illustrated*, March 1981, p. 10.

PRIVATE EYES AND POLICE

[1]The interview with Tareq S. Nabel took place in Amman, Jordan, Winter 1982.

²See "Yasser Arafat: The Man and His People," by Grace Halsell, in *The Link* (published by *Americans For Middle East Understanding*: New York, July/August 1982).

³See "The Palestinians," a series of articles by The Milwaukee *Journal* Editorial Page editor Sig Gissler. The articles appeared in the *Journal* Nov. 30 through Dec. 2, 1981.

⁴See Nahum Goldmann's interview in *Kurier*, "*Ich halte die Politik Israels für falsch*," published in Vienna, Austria, June 21, 1981.

⁵See *Time* magazine, "Key to a Wider Peace," April 14, 1980, pp. 38-56.

⁶Dr. Elwan's article on Arab women is available through the Arab Information Center, 747 Third Avenue, New York, NY 10017. The Center also published "Arab Women," by Nouha Alhegelan.

⁷The Department of State country papers provided the author with information on education. Also, additional information was obtained through personal interviews with U.S. Embassy personnel in selected Middle East nations.

⁸I visited on several occasion the *Hai Nazzal* Community Center in Amman.

⁹Personal correspondence with Dr. M.P. Ajalat, former president of the Arab-American Medical Association, June 10, 1981.

COMEDY

¹See *The New Republic* editorial, "The Other Anti-Semitism," March 1, 1980, pp. 5-7.

²See The Washington *Post*, "ABSCAM Ad-Libs," by Elisabeth Bumiller, Feb. 7, 1980, p. 3.

³See transcript of the *CBS Evening News*, May 22, 1980. Letter from Walter Cronkite to former *U.S. News and World Report* correspondent, dated June 17, 1980.

⁴See country paper on Oman, Dept. of State, Washington.

⁵See *React* magazine, published by Action for Children's Television (ACT), (Boston, MA, Summer 1980, p. 16).

⁶See *Time* magazine, "Mister Dugan Is Voted Out," March 19, 1979, p. 85.

⁷See James R. Baerg, "Television Programming Practice," in *The American Media and the Arabs*, edited by Hudson and Wolfe (Center For Contemporary Arab Studies at Georgetown University: Washington, D.C., 1980), pp, 45-48.

⁸See *The Washington Report on Middle East Affairs*, edited by John Law and published by The American Education Trust: Washington, D.C., February 7, 1981, p. 8.

DEATH OF A PRINCESS

¹*Death of a Princess* was telecast in the United States on May 12, 1980.

²See The St. Louis *Post-Dispatch*, May 8, 1983, p. 2A.

³See *The Evening Standard*, April 10, 1980, p. 1.

⁴See Charles Denton's comments in *The Daily Telegraph*, "ATV Has No

Regrets," by Peter Knight, April 11, 1980, pp. 1, 5.

[5]Newspapers in London that hyped *Princess* with headlines are *The Evening Standard*, April 8, 1980; *The Daily Express*, April 9, 1980 and *The Daily Mail*, April 10, 1980.

[6]See *The Guardian*, "Whitehall Still Fears Saudi Backlash" by John Hooper and Nikki Knewstub, April 11, 1980, p. 1.

[7]See *The Evening Standard*, "Sales Bonanza for 'Princess' Film," by Peter Wills, April 24, 1980.

[8]*Today*, May 9, 1980.

[9]*Good Morning, America*, May 8, 1980.

[10]Taped report for *Today* by NBC correspondent James Compton, from Cairo, Egypt, May 10, 1980.

[11]See The New York *Times*, "Saudi Protest Over Film Conveyed to Public TV by State Department," by Bernard Gwertzman, May 9, 1980, pp. 1, 9.

[12]The text of the letters from Acting Secretary of State Warren Christopher and Saudi Ambassador Alhegelan appeared in The New York *Times*, May 9, 1980, p. A10.

[13]See Ron Alridge's TV column in the Chicago *Tribune*, " 'Death of a Princess' Raises Mobil Oil's Ire," May 12, 1980.

[14]See "Public Broadcasting Act of 1967," Public Law 90-129, 90th Congress, S1160, Nov. 7, 1967.

[15]See St. Louis *Globe-Democrat*, "Death of a Princess Will Be Telecast Despite Pressure," May 9, 1980, p. 1.

[16]See *Broadcasting* Magazine, "Controversial 'Princess' Pulls Ratings for PBS," May 19, p. 73.

[17]See *Militant Islam* by Godfrey H. Jansen (Harper & Row: New York, 1980).

[18]See "Understanding Islam," by Harvey Cox, in *Atlantic* magazine, Jan., 1981, pp. 73-80.

[19]Contact the Middle East Institute in Washington for copies of Jerrold Fix's *The Middle East Institute Resource Guide for Teachers*.

[20]See " 'Princess' Film Typified Western Media Hypocrisy," by Victoria Schofield in *Voice*, London, England, June, 1980, p. 19.

[21]See transcript of *Death of a Princess*. Transcript provided by WGBH-TV Boston, for a nominal fee.

[22]See "Death Drama Stirs a Royal Row," in *Time* magazine, May 19, 1980, p. 46.

[23]See TV review of *Death of a Princess* by Nancy Banks-Smith, in *The Guardian*, April 10, 1980.

[24]Penelope Mortimer discussed the *Princess* program in a letter to *The New Statesman*. Mobil Oil published excerpts from Ms. Mortimer's letter in their national advertisement titled, "A New Fairy Tale."

[25]See transcript of the *NBC Nightly News*, May 12, 1980. Dr. Ajami's comments were read at the discussion program which immediately followed the airing of *Death of a Princess*.

DOCUMENTARIES

[1]Portions of this essay appeared in *Television Coverage of the Middle East*,

edited by William C. Adams (Ablex: Norwood, N.J., 1981).

[2]*60 Minutes*, "The Arabs Are Coming," Dec. 4, 1977.

[3]See *Oil Sheikhs*, by Linda Blandford (W.H. Allen & Co.: London, 1977).

[4]*60 Minutes*, "The 600 Million $ Man," Jan. 2, 1977.

[5]See "Foreigners Hold 4 Million Acres in the U.S.," by Seth S. King, in The New York *Times*, Oct. 3, 1979, p. 4.

[6]See "Foreign Investors Heed Call to 'Buy American' " by Peter Arnett, in the St. Louis *Globe-Democrat*, July 24, 1979, p. 15C.

[7]*NBC White Paper* on "Oil and American Power," Sept. 4, 1979.

[8]See *Arab Investors: Who They Are, What They Buy and Where, Vol. I.* by John Law (Chase World Information Corporation: New York, 1980).

[9]See "Saudi Marriage Mores Are Shaken as Women Seek a Stronger Voice," by Karen E. House, in *The Wall Street Journal*, June 1981, p. 1.

[10]*CBS Reports*, "The Saudis," Oct. 21, 1980.

[11]See "American First," by Harry Stein, *Esquire*, Feb. 1980, pp. 19-21.

[12]*Arabs and Israelis* series, seven half-hour documentaries telecast on PBS Feb. 3, 10, 19, 26 and March 5, 12, 19, 1975.

[13]*PBS*, "Israel and the Palestinians: Will Reason Prevail?" Jan. 7, 1981.

[14]*PBS*, "West Bank Story," March 25, 1981.

[15]See "Key to a Wider Peace," in *Time*, April 14, 1980, pp. 38-55.

[16]See "Israel's Unsettling Settlements," by Edward Hughes in *Reader's Digest*, May 1980, pp. 2-6.

[17]See "ABC's of Jewish Outposts in Occupied Territory," in *U.S. News and World Report*, Sept. 20, 1982, p. 28.

[18]*60 Minutes*, ". . .By What it Will Do to the Arabs," Feb. 15, 1981.

[19]*CBS Reports*, "The Palestinians," June 15, 1974.

[20]*ABC News Closeup*, "Terror in the Promised Land," Oct. 30, 1978.

[21]Michael J. Arlen, "ABC Visits the P.L.O.: The Sponsors Stay Home," *New Yorker*, Nov. 13, 1979, p. 140.

[22]Letter from Dolores Sura, CBS Director, Film and Video Licensing, Feb. 13, 1981.

[23]Letter from ABC-TV's Celeste Chin, April 13, 1981.

[24]*20/20*, "The Unholy War," April 2, 1981.

[25]See Sami Hadawi's book *Bitter Harvest* (New World Press: New York, 1967).

[26]See "The West Bank: A Hostage of History," by William Claiborne and Edward Cody. This two-part report on The West Bank appeared in The Washington *Post* and was reprinted by the Foundation for Middle East Peace (Washington, 1980).

[27]See "Blind Spot in the Middle East," a two-part article by John Weisman in *TV Guide*, Oct. 24, 1981.

[28]*20/20*, "If You Were The President," Aug. 6, 1981.

[29]See Uri Avneri's article, "What is a Terrorist?" in *Ha'olam Ha'zeh*, August 4, 1982.

[30]*20/20*, "Under The Israeli Thumb," Feb. 4, 1982.

[31]See " '20/20' Vision of Mideast: A Balanced Portrayal?" by Peter S. Boyer, in The Los Angeles *Times*, Feb. 4, 1982.

[32]*ABC News Closeup*, "Oh, Tell the World What Happened . . . ." Jan. 7, 1983.

[33]*CBS News Special Report*, "Death of a King: What Changes for the Arab World?" March 25, 1975. The special is available for "purchase only," $300.00.

[34]Collingwod letter, April 1, 1975.

[35]For more information on *Abraham's Children* contact the New York Foundation for the Arts, Sixth Floor, 5 Beekman Street, New York, NY 10038.

DISPELLING A STEREOTYPE

[1]The Japanese internment is discussed in *Prejudice, War, and the Constitution*, a book by Jacobus ten Broek, Edward N. Barnhart and Floyd M. Matson (Univ. of Calif. Press: Berkeley, 1954).

[2]See *TV Guide: The First Twenty-Five Years*, edited by Jay S. Harris (New American Library: New York, 1980).

[3]"Window Dressing on the Set: Women and Minorities in Television," (Report of the U.S. Commission on Civil Rights, Washington, August, 1977).

[4]See *Total Television* by Alex McNeil (Penguin Books: New York, 1980).

[5]See Erik Barnouw's *The Sponsor* (Oxford Univ. Press, 1978), pp. 101, 102. Prof. Barnouw's comments on the role of entertainment in his article "Documentary As A Subversive Activity," in *Television Quarterly*, Spring 1983, pp. 25-28.

[6]See "Public Opinion Sways Leaders, Study Maintains," in The St. Louis *Post-Dispatch*, Dec. 22, 1983, p. 10A.

[7]See "Hollywood and America: The Odd Couple," in *Public Opinion* magazine, pp. 54-58, Dec./Jan. 1983 issue. The article was written by Linda S. Lichter, S. Robert Lichter and Stanley Rothman.

[8]See *React* magazine, published by Action For Children's Television (ACT), Boston, MA: Summer, 1980, p. 16).

[9]Letter from *TV Guide*'s Andrew Mills to the author, Sept. 26, 1983.

[10]See *The View From Sunset Boulevard*, by Ben Stein (Basic Books: New York, 1979).

[11]See Art Peters' article, "What The Negro Wants From TV," in *TV Guide: The First Twenty-Five Years.*"

[12]See Neil Hickey's article, "What is TV Doing to Them," in *TV Guide: The First Twenty-Five Years.*

[13]See chapters on "Stereotyping in Our Culture" and "Choice of Scapegoats," in *The Nature of Prejudice*, by Gordon W. Allport (Addison-Wesley: Reading, MA: 1954).

[14]George Watson's comments made to Anisa Mehdi. See Mehdi's paper, "Through the Telephoto Lens: A Look at Arabs in Documentaries," supervised by Professor Judith Serrin, Columbia University Graduate School of Journalism, 1982.

Index

141